GUITAR AMPLIFIER
Encyclopedia

BRIAN TARQUIN

FOREWORD BY MICHAEL MOLENDA

ALLWORTH PRESS
NEW YORK

Allworth Press books may be purchased in bulk at special discounts for sales promotion, corporate gifts, fund-raising, or educational purposes. Special editions can also be created to specifications. For details, contact the Special Sales Department, Allworth Press, 307 West 36th Street, 11th Floor, New York, NY 10018 or info@skyhorsepublishing.com.

19 18 17 16 15   5 4 3 2 1

Published by Allworth Press, an imprint of Skyhorse Publishing, Inc.
307 West 36th Street, 11th Floor, New York, NY 10018.

Allworth Press® is a registered trademark of Skyhorse Publishing, Inc.®, a Delaware corporation.

www.allworth.com

Cover design by Mary Belibasakis
All photos by Erik Christian, Michael Howard, Ricky Restiano, and Crystal Scheidies
Cover photo credit: Erik Christian

Library of Congress Cataloging-in-Publication Data is available on file.

Print ISBN: 978-1-62153-499-0
Ebook ISBN: 978-1-62153-501-0

Printed in China

Table of Contents

foreword foreword
foreword foreword

Foreword

first knew a guitar amplifier could change the world when I heard of the "Little Green Amp." It was actually a 1962 Elpico, purchased that same year from a radio shop in Muswell Hill, London, by The Kinks guitarist Dave Davies. He originally viewed the tiny Elpico as an additional preamp for his Vox AC30, but along the way, some creative and mischievous angel whispered in his ear, and that amp became much more. Davies slashed the Elpico's speaker cone with a razor, plugged its output into the AC30, and the sound that was "You Really Got Me" was born. Miraculous!

As you can (hopefully) see, guitar amps are not just cold, boring circuit boxes for bringing the noise. Amps are the essential and mystical lovers of the electric guitar, and like with any object of desire, a lot of neural and emotional triggers have to fire off before a guitarist stares breathlessly and says, "You are the one." None of this, of course, has anything to do with reality. Amp tone is as subjective as it gets, so the "best" or "most appropriate" amp may be the one standing alone at the outside edges of the dance floor. You see, guitarists become obsessed with different amps for myriad reasons. Les Paul was always seeking the cleanest, truest, most transparent sound an amp could reproduce. Jimi Hendrix? Well, he didn't want that at all. Jimi wanted the beatific cacophony of a world gone mad with love, death, brotherhood, hate, peace, war, and everything written in the stars: in short, huge Marshall stacks spewing 110 decibels of grind. And then, there's everything in between, from mini amps, micro amps, practice amps, modeling amps, solid-state amps, tube amps, combos, half-stacks, boutique designs, and major-manufacturer builds. It's a jungle.

But whether you know what you're after and want to celebrate it, are looking to change your sound but don't know how, or are starting out on a quest for your own individual tone and need to know your options, *Guitar Amplifier Encyclopedia* will provide counsel and direction. By absorbing Brian Tarquin's survey of the past and present of guitar amplification, you'll be a better-informed player about what makes particular amps weave their sonic magic. It's also simply a super-fun book for amp freaks. So, go find your bliss.

Michael Molenda
Editor in Chief, *Guitar Player* magazine
30 September 2014

CHAPTER 1

Amplifier History

Bell 15RV Reverb combo made by Gibson with four inputs with one Jensen speaker

The Beginning

The one instrument in the world that needed to be amplified at the dawn of modern music was certainly the guitar. Just think of those noisy big band horns screaming their obnoxious notes, how the hell could a guy like Charlie Parker be heard over such a commotion? I'm a fan of classic films, and it always makes me laugh when I see a scene with a band leader and his baton waving at the orchestra and there in the corner is the lonely guitar player strumming away until he is blue in the face, but you can't hear a single note he's playing. I mean why is the guitar player even there if he can't be heard, just to keep quarter-note rhythm beats? It is absolutely no wonder why the amplifier was invented for the guitar! We can thank Benny Goodman for one thing, and that's integrating the talented black guitarist, Charlie Christian, which led to the electric guitar and amplifier. Whether you like the era's music or not, we certainly wouldn't have Hendrix, Clapton, Van Halen, or Satriani without Christian, or Gibson for that matter.

Amplification was first addressed for the electric guitar in the early 1930s for the Hawaiian guitarists who played this frying-pan-looking guitar on their lap. Companies like Rickenbacker, Gibson, Epiphone, and National tried to fulfill the need for volume by producing amps to accompany their Hawaiian guitars like the Rickenbacker A22, Gibson Roy Smeck, Gibson EH-185, Epiphone Model M, and Rickenbacker's Electro Tenor amplifier. You see, during the pre-World War II era, Rickenbacker had a large investment in the Hawaiian guitar market, as opposed to companies like National, Dobro, Gibson, and Epiphone who devoted their production to resonator and F-hole guitars. The Hawaiian-style guitar at the time of the late twenties through the thirties was a much more profitable market than the so-called Spanish neck guitars produced by Gibson.

Bandleaders of the twenties and thirties didn't take the guitar seriously in their music, looking upon it as a fad or a quirky instrument. Guitarists like Eddy Lang were the exception, accompanying singers like Ruth Etting in the 1932 film *A Regular Trouper* and Bing Crosby in the *The Big Broadcast of 1932*. Lang would use the original, acoustic version of the Gibson L-4 and L-5, before pickups were introduced. Then there was Eddie Durham, who was Count Basie's guitarist, who is noted as recording the world's first jazz electric guitar solo in 1938. He performed it on a Gibson ES-150 guitar with the Lester Young Kansas City Five. Ironically, the same year saw guitarists George Barnes with Big Bill Broonzy record electric guitar solos as well.

Whether it was timing or just fate, Benny Goodman, or all of the above, Charlie Christian was the poster boy for introducing the electric guitar into contemporary music. In Bonham, Texas, on July 29, 1916, Charlie was born into a musical family. Both his mother and father played the piano and trumpet as sound score in a local silent movie theatre. In 1918, after the family moved to Oklahoma City, Charlie began guitar lessons from his father. By 1928, he became heavily influenced by tenor saxophonist Lester Young; Charlie even scat sang Young's solos while playing the guitar. In fact T-Bone Walker was a childhood friend of Christian's, and they both took guitar lessons from Ralph "Big-Foot Chuck" Hamilton in the earlier thirties. Moreover, a chance meeting with Eddie Durham in 1937 changed the course of Charlie's fate, because he was so influenced by Eddie's guitar playing. Soon after that meeting Christian went out and bought a Gibson ES-150 with the accompanying amp and started to woodshed. Within a year Charlie was getting local recognition in the Midwest as a hometown hero. Christian was even playing the difficult styles of Django Reinhardt's "St. Louis Blues" solo, verbatim.

By 1939 Charlie got the attention of producer John Hammond. With Gibson ES-150 guitar and amp in hand, Charlie was set up for an audition with Benny Goodman by Hammond. In typical Goodman fashion, he was not impressed at the comping style of Christian, but later was blown away at Charlie's solo ability to keep up with him note for note. This was the year everything changed for Christian as he went on to record landmark songs with the Goodman Sextet, Septet and Orchestra, the Lionel Hampton Orchestra, and the historic Carnegie Hall jazz concert. Standout recordings of "Solo Flight" and "Honeysuckle Rose," made Charlie a legend and a new master of jazz guitar. Then in 1940 Christian went up to Harlem and participated in jam sessions at Minton's Playhouse. He jammed with such future greats as Thelonius Monk and Dizzy Gillespie, forming the sketches of bebop that would appear a decade later in New York. He even bought a Gibson amp to become the house amp for the playhouse. However, like great musical artists Jimi Hendrix, Jim Morrison, and Randy Rhoads, he died young of tuberculosis in 1942. So the world was deprived of any great solo records that were surely to come. But he laid the foundation for the electric guitar amplifier and ironically died the same year Jimi Hendrix was born, so one great guitar spirit passes to another!

Early Amp Designers

Established instrument companies formed in the nineteenth century started to produce amplifiers when the new pre-World War II electronic craze began. This would help many companies create a strong foothold in the new market. Here is a list of some of the early companies that were involved in producing guitar amps.

Harmony: Wilhelm Schultz, a European immigrant, formed Harmony in 1892. The Chicago company became one of the largest manufacturers of guitars and amps. By 1916 Sears Roebuck bought Harmony, and in 1923 Harmony's annual sales rose to 250,000 units. The company continues to be strong today and stands behind its proud heritage.

Supertone: From 1914 to 1941 Supertone was the Sears brand name for its musical instruments. It wasn't until the forties that Sears switched the name to Silvertone, which people are familiar with today. Keep in mind that Sears never manufactured the amps themselves; they were always outsourced to other companies.

Jackson-Guldan: A violin company based in Columbus, Ohio, from the 1920s to 1960s. It produced lap steels accompanied by small tube amps.

Epiphone: This is a story that dates all the way back to the Ottoman Empire in Europe. Epaminondas, son of a Greek immigrant, apprenticed with his father in instrument making and at age twenty-two found himself in charge of the family business when his father passed away in America. They had a showroom on 14th Street in NYC, which became a hangout spot for New York musicians like Les Paul and Harry Volpe, who would jam there on Saturday afternoons. By 1935 Epiphone became one of the greatest guitar manufactures, so it is no surprise Epiphone offered amps early on in the thirties. Epiphone sold amps into the mid-seventies and then reintroduced them in 1991 with the EP series.

National/Valco: Like Epiphone's, these amps date back to the thirties. But it was in the sixties when National introduced a modern group of amps to accompany their new Res-O-Glas space-age guitars. Then by 1968 they revamped the amp line with large vertical and horizontal piggyback models. One of the last amps was the National GA 950 P Tremolo/Reverb piggyback.

Bogen: In 1932 David Bogen founded this New York company and manufactured a number of electronic products like the small guitar combo tube amps. Some of the models were the GA-5 and the GA-20 including PA systems. During the Rockabilly era, these amps were well favored by guitarists.

Kalamazoo: As you guessed it—these amps were manufactured by Gibson; however, they were considered low-budget amps from 1933 to 1942. The name later appeared on amps manufactured in the late sixties.

Guyatone: This company started producing amps in the forties that accompanied their lap steel guitars called Guya. It made a host of amplifiers including Marco Polo, Winston, Kingston, Kent, LaFayette, and Bradford brands.

Vivi-Tone: In 1933 former Gibson employee Lloyd Loar, along with some coworkers, formed the company in Kalamazoo. It produced small amps to be used with early electric guitars.

Supro: The National Dobro Company built these amps in conjunction with Valco as budget amplifiers. But when Jimmy Page got ahold of this cheaply made amp, we were shown a Whole Lotta Love! In recent years the Supro name has been resurrected, offering reissues of the old models.

Electar Amp: These amps are sparse on the market and were only manufactured in the late thirties. The early models, such as the Model C, Model M, Super AC-DC, and Special AC-DC were compact with 1x8" speakers. The later model, Electar introduced the twelve-inch speaker with larger cabinets for the combos.

Audiovox: This was a Seattle company formed in 1935 by Paul Tutmarc. Like many manufacturers of the time, it produced electric lap steels, guitars, and—of course—amps to accompany its other products.

Dickerson: In 1937 the Dickerson brothers formed this company to manufacture electric lap steel guitars and amps. In those days, lap steel guitars were sold with their matching amps. They also made instruments for companies like the Oahu Company, to be rebranded. Finally after World War II Dickerson was sold and renamed Magna Electronics, which became Magnatone.

Selmer: Formed by World War I veteran Ben Davis in 1928, this company was on the cutting edge in Britain. During the early thirties, it produced amplifiers and became the first UK musical company to do so. It was the strongest distributor of amps, which lasted well into the British Invasion.

Premier: In 1938 the Peter Sorkin Music Company in NYC manufactured these amps. It introduced very small, radio-sized amplifiers by the end of the thirties. Post World War II, it created the brand name Multivox, which produced guitar amps until the eighties. The fifties and sixties would see more ornate amp designs featuring dark-brown and light-tan coverings, along with handsome wood grains.

Hanburt: Harvey M. Hansen started producing electric Hawaiian guitars in Seattle and, like many of his contemporaries, sold amps with the guitars as a set. These amps were typically made out of wood and small in nature.

Danelectro: In 1946 Nathan Daniel founded this diverse musical-instrument company in New Jersey. He started with building Sherwood amps for the department-store retailer Montgomery Ward and went on to supplying Sears with their Silvertone. Nathan produced his own amps under the company name and the brand SS Maxwell. The Evets Corporation reintroduced the Danelectro brand in the nineties.

Alamo: In 1949 the conglomerate of Charles Eilenberg, Milton Fink, and Southern produced a variety of amps all the way until the eighties.

Webcor: During the forties, the Webster-Chicago Company was mostly known for building recording equipment. However, it also produced small amplifiers intended for vinyl turntables and PA systems.

Masco: In the span from the forties into the fifties the Mark Alan Sampson Company of New York built an array of portable amp combos. They also manufactured tube PA systems for Blues harp players.

Massie: Before the formation of Fender during the forties Ray Massie worked with Leo Fender repairing instruments. Ray was Leo's main repairman and amp designer; he would work for Fender later.

Flot-A-Tone: This Wisconsin company in the forties and fifties produced various musical amps for both guitar and accordion. It is well known for having great tremolo systems, and country guitarists like Ry Cooder are big fans of these little amps.

Framus: A German company that manufactured amp heads, combos, and cabinets. It began in 1946 as an acoustic-instrument company, but then added electric instruments in the fifties. Like other brands we've seen, it was revived in the nineties.

Geoff Gray guitar collection at Far & Away Studios, Boulder, Colorado

The Vintage Collector

I've known Geoff for over two decades, and he is a die-hard vintage instrument and amp collector. I started out recording with Geoff in 1990 and soon became his assistant engineer at his recording studio, Far & Away, in New York. He was a mentor to me in those days, and I learned quite a lot from him about recording. He even took me to Les Paul's house back in the day to hang with the man himself and eat popcorn and experience the endless museum of guitars, amps, recording gear, and stories that Les had to offer. Yes, I received quite an education from my days with Geoff, so I couldn't write a book about amps without having Geoff share some of his immense knowledge.

Geoff has been involved in music recording since the early seventies. As he explains, "We currently have a wonderful studio in Colorado and share our forty-some tube amps with our clients. It's great to have this huge palette of tone to choose from when working on a project. The first amp I ever bought was a Sears Silvertone 1484. I found the receipt about a year ago. It cost $166.00. I used that in my high school and college bands. I pretty much ignored it and lusted after a Marshall stack. It's a lesson learned regarding full circles. I just replaced my long-gone original with another 1484, and it sounds unbelievable. I have a Marshall stack that seldom gets used. And so it goes. In the sixties we all had a life-changing experience with the release of the first John Mayall album with Eric Clapton, using his Les Paul through the Marshall eighteen-watt "Bluesbreaker" amp. Concurrently, Hendrix's *Are You Experienced* album sound took our heads off. The lead guitarist in my college band had a Les Paul TV Model that he coupled to an old Vox AC 30. That sound has never left me. It opened my mind to the endless possibilities of tone and put me on a quest that seems to never end. I "outgrew" the Marshall-stack era about the same time I was introduced to Tweed Fender amps, specifically the 4x10"

Bassman. I have had four of them, and they are life changing. That led to a Tweed Deluxe and the entire line of fifties Fender Tweeds. I still record a ragged 1954 Super that came from an accordion player in Rhode Island. We kid that he must have dragged it behind his car to every gig. It still sounds incredible. I brought a 1959 Champ to Les Paul's house one night, and he liked it so much he asked me to find him one, which I subsequently did."

Geoff reflects how he became a collector of vintage amps, "What started me collecting was that search for better and more varied tone. I still discover amps that were not on my radar. We just acquired a 1964 Selmer Tru Voice Bass n Treble 50 Croc Era. I'm in shock. Where have these been my entire career? It's funny how we've had access to so many great amps here at the studio and still discover gems about every couple of months. The investment aspect of vintage amps can't be denied either. Many have outpaced other investment instruments. It's a side bonus. It's nice knowing that you can use your investment and increase in value. If you're out buying a guitar from a private individual, always ask if they have any old amps. You might be surprised at what might be in the basement. It pays to be educated on what is original and what is not. I would highly advise having an amp-repair guru close at hand. Sometimes mint old amps need a ton of work, and some of the rattiest looking things are stellar."

At Far & Away Studios, Geoff has seen a lot of amps, and he explains how they vary.

There are so many variables in electric guitar recording, for instance, the guitar, the amp, the volume, the room, the mic, the preamp, the tape, or the convertors. There are so many technical reasons that amps sound differently from one another in the studio that it becomes an involved discussion. You have variations in power tube types, rectifier types, amount of

Far & Away's 1963 Watkins Dominator V-shaped amp

negative feedback used, and, of course, speaker type. Ken Fisher (Trainwreck Amps) once pointed out to me that single-speaker amps have a certain purpose. He said Billy Gibbons of ZZ Top used a 100-watt Celestion on some of the early stuff. When you listen, it does sound very direct and focused. That was intentional. We use one twelve-inch or one ten-inch amp for that feel. Our current studio favorites are 1960 through 1964 Harmony H 305 or 306 amps. One channel has been slightly modded to produce more gain. I like two or four speakers for many tracks, because the spill from the other speaker or speakers bleeds onto the mic and makes the sound a little fuller. Sometimes it's two mics, one on each speaker. Laws of physics dictate that you must keep the second mic three times the distance that the first mic is from the source. For example, if the mic is six inches from the grill, the second mic would have to be eighteen inches to the side of the first mic. This assumes they're both six inches from the grill. This ensures phase alignment. We use distance mics often as well. Ours are generally ribbon mics and dynamic mics. It wasn't until I started working with Steve Carey of Fluxtone speakers that I realized how much of the sound of an amp is directly related to the speakers. I always knew they were important, but now I realize they are probably 60 to 70 percent of the sound. We've done a bunch of comparisons switching amps and speakers to realize this. There are some cool YouTube videos of Brad Paisley demoing the

Fluxtone-equipped amps. They change the amp recording paradigm significantly.

How does Geoff feel about digital modeling amps?

I have a real problem mixing modeling amps and even solid-state amps. There is something that I would term "front-to-back imaging" that is missing from those sources. It's hard to describe, but anyone can hear the difference when comparing them to a tube amp. EQ never seems to help either. My most glaring example was during the recording of a death metal band with identical Boogie 8x12" stacks, one powered by a Marshall and one by a MOSFET head. I stood in front of both to make sure they were the same level, and there were no pedals. I used the same mic and the same mic preamp. I recorded them to tape. There was a large gobo between them. In the mix there was nothing I could do to make the solid-state amp equal the depth and quality of the Marshall. The guys were playing the same parts panned left and right. Had the Marshall not been in the mix, the solid-state amp might have sounded OK, but it sure sounded weak against the tubes. We just panned them closer to center and moved on. Modeling is sure a cool idea but has a way to go to be convincing.

Les Paul

Having been close friends with Les Paul, I wanted to see how much Les was involved with the evolution of guitar amplification. Geoff explains,

This is a great question! Les wasn't about amps for recording. I just found out recently from Tom Doyle, Les's long-time friend and luthier, that Les started to use low-impedance pickups in 1952. The idea was to avoid guitar amps altogether. With this style pickup, you can record directly into the console. No direct box needed. These were humbucking low impedance pickups, by the way. He never thought of patenting humbucking pickups, because the technology for humbucking transformers had been around since the twenties. It was public domain.

Les was always searching for sustain, but clean sustain. He also was searching for the same volume output for every note on the guitar. We all benefitted from the sustain requirement, but it turned out to be amp distortion. During the recording of the Chester and Lester album, Les told me how it worked. He used an amp to rehearse in the studio with the band. At the same time, the engineer was receiving the low impedance output from Les's guitar. I remember him saying, "If the guy can't get levels by then he shouldn't be in there recording." When it was time to do a take, the headphones came out, and Les put the amp on standby. Thus what actually got recorded was the 600-ohm low impedance signal from Les's guitar. Les used Fender Twin Reverbs a lot. His original amp was a 1951 Fender Super given to him by Leo Fender the same time Leo gave him the famed Nocaster. I now own that old amp. The Fender logo on the front was removed, and it says Gibson on the top panel. Les wanted to stay true to his endorsement. When I was helping Les with gigs in the seventies he was using a Gibson amp. The large logo covered up the hidden part of the Les Paulverizer. It can be seen in The Wizard of Waukesha movie. At Fat Tuesdays and the Iridium, Les was using Fender Twins for all those shows if memory serves me correctly.

Geoff reminisces on how he met Les Paul:

In 1973 I returned home to find a note from my roommate saying, "Old man called about your guitar." I was running an ad in the venerable Want Ad Press for a 1956 Gibson J160E with a Les Paul pickup. I placed the return call, and the voice at the other end asked me to describe the instrument. I said it had a P90 Les Paul pickup at the base of the neck. He cut in "It's not a P90." I fired back that it was, but that it just didn't have a cover on it. The response was an in-depth rebuttal regarding how it was optimized as an acoustic pickup, etc. I said, "How do you know all this stuff?" He shot back "I'm Les Paul." Without faltering, I said, "I have so much to learn from you … can we ever meet?" Les said, "What are you doing now, here's where I live." I said, "I'm grabbing my car keys as we speak." One half hour later, that ubiquitous left-hand shake started a journey for me that changed my life for the better. This led me to buy my first 4-track Ampex tape machine from Les. That action propelled me into my career and a thousand more questions to ask Les about the recording process.

Les was much more accessible at that point in his life than in later years when he was "rediscovered." I got to be somewhat of an insider, spending many late nights with him, his son Russ, Ralph the maintenance guy, and Wally, Les's sweet brother-in-law. I accompanied Les to many shows: Storyville, Saratoga Performing Arts Center with B. B. King, the MOMA gig with George Benson, Bucky Pizzarelli, Gabor Szabo, college gigs for the filming of *The Wizard of Waukesha*, and the early Ramada Inn gigs. It was usually just Les and me driving to the gig in the old Chevy, CB radio code name, the Red Wagon. Les loved people and was one of the most humorous guys I've ever met. He was a raconteur extraordinaire. After a late night in his Mahwah kitchen, where Les held court and served popcorn, I would wake up with sore abs, as if I'd done two hundred sit-ups, and then remember how much we'd laughed. An audience of one or three thousand is still an audience. Vaudeville taught Les well.

Historically before Les, when recording a performance in the studio, it was captured live with no options for overdubs. But Les claimed, "I'm going back in time to change that note, add a harmony guitar part, and double Mary's vocal." Everyone said, "Impossible!" "Can't be done." Words that Les ate up and spit out. Even before tape machines, when recordings were made direct to lathe in his garage, Les had the idea of bouncing from one lathe to another (made from Cadillac flywheels) and concurrently adding additional parts to the original recording. Les had scores of thoughts. In 1957 he wrote an academic paper for the Audio Engineering Society that suggested recording with light (the CD) and the Les Paulverizer that allows queueing up of prerecorded background tracks to play over in live performances. In the forties he suggested the invention of the fretted bass, the headless guitar, and the solid-body electric guitar. And of course in 1953 he came up with the idea for the multitrack tape machine.

Gibson

Gibson amplifiers predate any Fender or Vox on the market and capture those pre-solid guitar body tones, as we saw earlier with Charlie Christian's ES-150. Gibson has a rich history that can be traced back to the nineteenth century. Guitar amplifiers have become so integrated and intertwined with twentieth-century rock stars, it's astonishing that it all started in the 1890s in the workshop of Orville Gibson. The whole reason he created the carved-arch top for the mandolin and guitars was to make them louder. The obvious evolution was to move with technology and eventually build amps. So the company Gibson was formed by a group of businessmen in Kalamazoo, Michigan in 1902, and was called Gibson Mandolin-Guitar Mfg. Co., Ltd.

As loud as the acoustic models Gibson was producing at the time were (such as the L5), they

The Gibson Bell 15RV Reverb even has an accordion volume knob.

were still all drowned out by the horns, piano, and drums onstage. So it was a natural move to electrify the guitar in the 1930s and build an accompanying amp. So in 1936 Gibson was the first major manufacturer to release an electric guitar, the ES-150, boasting one single-coil pickup. It sold with a matching amplifier as a package for $150.00, consequentially becoming the ES-150.

It wasn't until after World War II that Gibson went into high gear for amp production. Under the auspicious Ted McCarty, Gibson was propelled onto the amp market for the post-war music scene. These models started out small in production and included the BR-1, 2, 3, and the BR-1. But by the early fifties Gibson was cranking out a reportedly ten thousand amps per year—wow, that's a lot of tubes! Gibson amps were inherently warmer-sounding than Fenders and had a fuller tonal pattern overall. Although the solid-state transistor was invented at

Seventies Gibson G10 Solid State with a killer-sounding tremolo takes an MXR Distortion Plus nicely!

Bell Labs in the forties, the technology didn't show up in amps until the sixties, mostly because of the reluctance of the industry.

There has always been this huge argument over tubes vs. solid-state, which is a bunch of hogwash. I have to say, even though I'm a tube-amp guy, I have heard some great solid-state amps. It all has to do with the player's hands! I have a cheaper G-10 from the seventies, and it has one hell of a great-sounding tremolo. Only recently did people make a huge fuss over this technology. In the seventies, you couldn't give away a tube amp because everything was transistor. The thought behind this was that tube technology was old and broken down, where transistors were smaller and made for lighter amps to carry around to gigs. Listen, I had a solid-state Yamaha G-Series 212 combo with push-pull knobs for boost, and it sounds great with a distortion pedal. In fact, people used to mistake the tone for a Marshall. How many bands have I had to sit through and listen to the guitarists with a half-stack tube Marshall sound like dog poo? The instrument will only sound as good as what you put through it, plain and simple. In fact Gibson built one of the first amplifiers that combined tube-power amps with solid-state preamps, something we see in place today with certain brands.

CHAPTER 2

Fender, King of Amps

Innovation

Who would have thought the guitar amp that changed the world and sparked the six-string revolution in the 1960s was born out of a radio repair shop in Fullerton, California? To understand the origins of the electric guitar and amp, you have to know the times in which it was created. In the 1930s, Hawaiian lap steel guitars were in vogue, so many instrument manufacturers like Rickenbacker on the West Coast were producing these models with accompanying amps. Leo was no different, and he dove into a partnership with Clayton Orr "Doc" Kauffman, who had worked at Rickenbacker making lap steel guitars. The partnership was called

K & F Manufacturing Corporation in 1945. But this was a short-lived partnership; the two split in 1946, and Leo went on to form Fender Electric Instrument Company in 1947. The first amplifier Fender made was called the Princeton, an extremely archaic amp with no controls because it was sold with an accompanying guitar by the same name that had the amp-volume control built on it. Then came the Deluxe (Model 26), which featured a 1x10" speaker and five tubes housed in a simple wooden cabinet nicknamed "Woodie."

Leo started to experiment with the idea of a solid body, to reduce feedback when amplified. Manufacturers like Gibson, Rickenbacker,

1951 Fender Super Amp, owned by Les Paul and now owned by Geoff Gray at Far & Away Studios

This 1952 Fender Tweed Deluxe in pristine shape looks like it just came off of the assembly line.

1952 Fender Tweed Deluxe has two instrument inputs, one microphone input, and three control knobs.

1952 Fender Tweed Deluxe: a back view to show the simplicity of the design

National, and Epiphone all made various types of hollow-body guitars for years, but there was a desire from musicians to have a solid-body guitar, after all a man named Lester William Polsfuss (Les Paul) was doing this in New York. So by 1950 Leo had his first solid-body guitar in production, the Esquire, later the Broadcaster, and ultimately the Telecaster. This same time saw the introduction of the Champion amplifier line with glorious tweed tolex and chrome finishing. Then came the breakthrough year of 1951 when Leo designed the Precision Bass. Why is this so important in an amp book? Well, what came next to go along with the new P bass should interest you greatly: the iconic Bassman amp. By the end of that year Leo did it again, with the design of the Fender Twin 2x12" amp.

Guitars & Amps

Then, in 1954, it happened. The guitar that would change rock 'n' roll forever and give the beautiful sound of dive bombs: the Stratocaster was born!

Fender 1959 Bandmaster sporting 3x10" speakers and tweed tolex finish

This gorgeous, sleek beauty featured a tremolo bar for all sorts of pitch effects, six bridge saddles, three single-coil pickups, pick guard, and a new recessed input jack on the face of the body. Everything about the Strat was new and advanced, yet such a classic that it stays with us to this day. During this same time a new addition came to the amp lineup, the Bandmaster, powered by two-6L6's. This featured

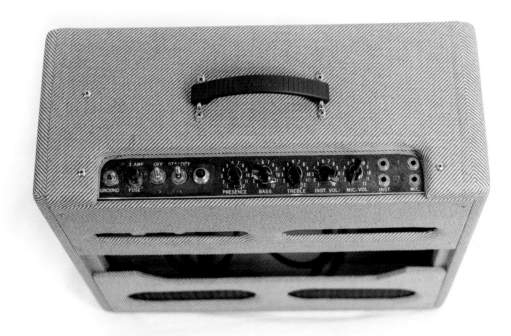

Fender 1959 Bandmaster showing the chrome top plate with four inputs for both instrument and microphone

the upgraded tone-control circuit similar to the Twin, with separate bass and treble knobs. The new Bandmaster featured such controls as instrument volume, microphone volume, bass, and treble with three input jacks—two for instruments and one for a microphone, plus a Jensen P15-N speaker.

Designed for those ax men who needed more amp power in the late forties, Leo came up with an amp line simply called the Professional. They were built in larger cabinets than the Deluxe or Princeton models and used the best materials available at the time. First they beefed up the tubes to include two metal 6L6's, pumping out an extraordinary twenty-five watts through a Jensen fifteen-inch field coil speaker, a lot of wattage for the time. Input channels used cathode-biased 6SJ7 tubes, a 5U4 rectifier tube, and a 6N7 twin triode tube for a phase inverter. This new Professional series was responsible for introducing tweed tolex to Fender amps. Before such amps as the Deluxe, there were just wooden boxes with no covering. By the end of the forties Fender produced the Dual Professional, which quickly morphed into the Super. The Super went through many changes through the years, but it wasn't until the early sixties that it came of age, when Fender released the Super Reverb, one of my

Fender 1954 Tweed Deluxe with extension cabinet viewed from the back showing that beautiful aged tweed

Fender 1954 Tweed Deluxe with extension cabinet: straight to the point, simple, and lightweight!

Mid-seventies Super Reverb and cut-down Fender Twin Reverb head, plenty of tone there to go around!

Gold sparkle-covered Fender Princeton reissue featuring tremolo effect and six control knobs

favorite Fender amps of all time. Just think of that fantastic tone Stevie Ray Vaughan captured in the studio with his Super Reverb. I've recorded many of these amps in the studio, and it's amazing how good they sound after all of these years of being banged around by guitar players.

By 1959, Leo released his "finest electric guitar," the Jazzmaster, which was a much flashier guitar at the time. It had a separate rosewood fingerboard glued on top of a maple neck, a new floating tremolo system, a gold pick guard made from aluminum, slider selector switchers, unique body shape, and an enlarged headstock. The one downside of the guitar was those large, unshielded pickups, which picked up a lot of hum and noise onstage and in the studio. By this point the Fender Bassman had gone through some major changes by switching out the 1x15" speaker to using 4x10"

speakers. It also swapped one of the second 12AY7s for a 12AX7 to add more gain and replaced the 6L6 power tubes with 5881 tubes. On top of that they added more tone controls, so the amps could be more versatile.

Another exciting addition to the lineup was the Tremolux, armed with two 6V6 power tubes and an onboard oscillator creating that sought-after tremolo effect. This period also introduced the Harvard, a small practice amp that was a cross between the Princeton and the Deluxe. The Harvard was powered by two 6V6s feeding a ten-inch speaker in a tiny cabinet. Then came the Vibrolux, which also had a ten-inch speaker, and much like the Tremolux, it featured tremolo. It came with four control knobs: volume, tone, speed, and depth, plus three input jacks. Then came the Vibrasonic, which marked a big change in design and laid out the

The Fender 1965 Princeton Reverb "Pink Paisley" is sure to turn ears as well as eyes.

controls on a slanted angle on the front of the amp, so musicians could easily see the controls and make necessary adjustments. The amp also featured two separate channels, Normal and Vibrato, each having separate volume and tone controls. This design change became the standard for all Fender amps moving forward, and the Vibrasonic became the flagship amp for Fender in 1960.

The Sixties

By the early sixties Fender was constantly updating and adding new amps to its roster. The Concert series was one of these amps that found its way to showrooms in the early sixties. It was a beast of an amp with 4x10" Jensen speakers, two 6L6 power tubes, five 7025 tubes, two 6L6GC tubes, and the new Fender tremolo circuitry. Another collector's favorite is the Showman from the early sixties

featuring a separate head and cabinet, something very revolutionary for Fender at the time. This configuration is always associated with British manufacturers like Vox and Marshall. The head and cabinet could be secured together by special attachments, and the cabinet had those annoying metal legs that swung out, enabling the amp and cabinet to tilt backward. These metal legs were equipped on Fender combos like the Twin and the Super Reverb.

But Fender's hallmark amp was the Vibroverb, and like the name implies, it featured Fenders new reverb circuitry. In fact it was Fender's first amp featuring reverb, and it became the sound of the sixties, especially for Surf music. Other Fender amp models followed suit and were renamed as the Twin Reverb, Super Reverb, and Deluxe Reverb. Reverb in amplifiers always bewilders me because the amps never sound very good. It's the same stale spring reverb tone, and if you knock into the amp, you hear a loud bang that echoes through the room. I can't imagine why anyone in modern times would even care if there was reverb in an amp. I've recorded quite a few amps, and I never record an amp with reverb on it; the studio has so many superior-sounding effects you can use. I think you have to consider the times, for the sixties this was a huge progression in sound that would lead to even better tones.

CBS Era

This takes us to 1965, when CBS purchased the company for $13 million from Leo. Fender had firmly established itself as the top guitar and amplifier manufacturer in America. At the time, the sum made history as the highest purchase price for a single music manufacturer. So ended an era of craftsman building and ushered in a new period of mass manufacturing. Two generations collided, the old Fender craftsmen who had no formal training

Fender 1957 Tweed Champ: great for recording blues harp!

Fender 1957 Tweed Champ: very simple, one control knob and two inputs, what more could you ask for in the fifties?

and built each amp by hand, and the new college engineers who believed in the bottom dollar of profits from mass production. As with many large companies that acquired new businesses, CBS poured money into Fender to achieve guitar and

amp manufacturing on a large scale. So came the release of the practice amp the Bronco, a simple, solid-state amp for the beginning musician. I must say the Vibro Champ sounded much better than the Bronco for having a small eight-inch speaker. Under the new CBS management, things for Fender started to deteriorate with such amps as the Super Six Reverb, Music Master Bass, and some of their solid-state amp releases like the Dual Showman, Twin Reverb, Bassman, Super Reverb, Pro Reverb, Vibrolux Reverb, and the Deluxe Reverb. This was CBS management at work, thinking people would buy their popular amps in a solid-state version.

This was also the period of the Blackface amps, produced from 1964 to 1967, that Fender started before the sale to CBS. Under new management, the faceplates changed to read "Fender Musical Instruments." It was in 1968 when the changes were made to the cosmetics and the new Silverface

Fender 1974 Super Reverb, one of the most amazing-sounding amplifiers in the Fender lineup!

Era took hold. The subtle differences were the blue lettering on the silver knob plate and other small details that certain people obsessed over. But the real, noticeable change was in 1973 when it added a master volume knob that doubled as a boost knob when pulled out. The Silverface production went right into the eighties until the Rivera Era began. In the mid-seventies, Fender revived the Blackface cosmetics designed by Ed Jahns. The result was an extraordinarily loud Super Twin and Super Twin Reverb that had a modified overdrive circuit with active tone controls. Can you say Cat Scratch Fever? Ted Nugent used these Twin Reverbs at ear-bleeding volumes in the seventies stacking them a mile high behind him onstage.

Touring in the nineties, performing at various jazz festivals, I always requested a Fender Blackface Twin Reverb reissue—or the real thing if possible—with a Marshall 4x12" cabinet. I'd piggyback the Twin on the Marshall that gave so many tonal possibilities. The Blackface has the right amount of sag from the power supply and a warm, cushy, fat tone when you add a Tube Screamer. Their tone comes from AB763 circuit, as it's called. They use an astonishing four 6L6GC output tubes and six preamp tubes—two 12AT7 tubes and four 7025/12AX7 types. I always found the Vibrato channel warmer and easier to push into a warm, brown tone. I like the ability to overdrive the output tubes, not just the preamp, so I tend to like the Blackface. On the seventies master volume, it is virtually impossible to overdrive those output tubes without going deaf, but that is why some Jazz guys love it. I also had this master volume Twin Reverb from the seventies that was cut down just to be a head: wonderful vibrato tones that you'd expect from Fender, nice clean tone for days.

By the seventies the question loomed: Were Fender's best days behind it or could it recover and be influential again? Keep in mind that originally Fender catered to the music of country western in the forties and fifties, but by 1970 the music scene had changed considerably. Although Fender was in its amplifier heyday during this period, the music was swept up in the British Invasion. For instance,

1970s Fender Twin Head cut down from a combo, beat up but still produces shimmering cleans and lush tremolo tones

bands like The Who, Jeff Beck, Eric Clapton with Cream, and Led Zeppelin were using Marshall amps over Fender. The playing field for Fender changed by the seventies. Also keep in mind it was an instrument manufacturer as well as building amplifiers, whereas Marshall was solely producing amplifiers. Inevitably time would answer this question, and yes Fender was able to eventually bounce back, but it would take another decade.

A Change Is Comin'

The eighties for Fender were tough as it tried to keep up with amp companies like MESA/Boogie and Marshall. It recruited amp designer Paul Rivera to do a makeover on its amplifiers with the new II Series models, like the Twin Reverb II and Deluxe Reverb II. The amps retained their classic, clean tone; however, Rivera added a high-gain voicing in the amp to compete with amps like MESA. Remember, these were the hair band days—*yikes*! Unfortunately, they never took off for the targeted market, and loyal fans of the Fender were alarmed to say the least. After the "Rivera Era" came the dreaded "Red Knob Era." These amps were manufactured under CBS management and had push-pull, high-gain controls and boost pots. They contained

printed circuit boards and tube technology that was hated by studio techs for the difficulty to service. If the Rivera amp era wasn't popular at the time, these were even less popular. What resulted was a bunch of pissed-off loyal Fender users. The final insult was the bloody ugly M-80 amp heads and cabs upholstered in gray carpet with high gain and effects built in like the dreaded CHORUS. Talk me down off the ledge, Spock! So Fender wisely looked to the amplifiers of the past that made them famous and reissued them.

In 1985 Fender was purchased from CBS by William Schultz, the company president, with a group of employees and investors. This would usher an entire era of rebirth for Fender—the Lazarus Effect, I like to call it. I distinctly remember being a teenager in the late seventies and going to Manny's NYC to buy a new amplifier. I looked at a lot of amps, and none of them were Fenders. In fact, they had become so out of vogue it wasn't even a option. On top of that, tubes were considered old hat; most manufacturers were making solid-state amps. The salesman told me that Fenders had become so poorly made, he encouraged me to buy a Japanese amp, because it was superior sounding, better made,

The 1990s Fender Prosonic Head finally mastered the overdrive tone!

Fender's unmistakable logo makes you feel good when you see it, like the street you grew up on!

and more affordable. Then came the eighties and all bets were off, nothing but a Marshall!

So by the early nineties Fender was back on track, introducing models like the Pro Junior Blues, the Junior Blues, and the Deluxe Blues DeVille. These amps were at the perfect price point for musicians to buy a tube amp without breaking the bank. At this point the affordable tube-amp market had no competition, so Fender was able to cash in on this untapped market. This was around the time it opened up the Custom Shop to deliver the high-end amps to people who desired to spend the money. The Tonemaster and Vibro King are examples of Custom Shop amps. They have a very retro feel and tone, boasting hand-to-hand wiring and tube tremolo like the old Vibrasonic, typical of retro Fenders. However, my two favorite modern Fenders are the Prosonic and the EVH 5150III 50-Watt head. Fender finally got the high-gain stage right with these two amps.

The Eddie Van Halen 5150III 50-Watt has a resonance knob on the back, which sounds exactly like my modded Marshall. But the cool thing about the EVH amp is I can get a beautiful clean channel with a click of the pedal. Thank you very much! Two JJ 6L6 tubes power it with a preamp section consisting of seven JJ ECC83 tubes. It has three channels: Clean, Crunch, and Lead with a Master Presence. Channel: 1 and 2 controls are as follows: Gain, Low, Mid, High, and Volume. Channel 3's controls are: Gain, Low, Mid, High, and Volume, plus the Master Resonance Control is on the rear panel. There is also a handy four-button remote switcher, and it can be hooked up via MIDI input to control channels and effects loop with any MIDI device. The 100-watt version is much the same; however, there is no resonance control, which to me makes the fifty-watter that much better and more valuable. You can purchase the matching 5150III 4x12" cabinet with four 12-inch Celestion; G12EVH, these feature Eddie's signature speakers.

Fender Blues Junior III Limited Edition featuring gorgeous wood finish

Fender Blues Junior III Limited Edition backside, wonderfully crafted with a wood handle

Fender continues to use guitar star royalty to sell amps like the Eric Clapton Signature Twinolux based on the classic Twin model 5E8-A from the fifties. Fender added Tremolo circuitry with speed and intensity controls. As you would expect, no holds barred with hand-wired tube circuitry on the eyelet board. This bad boy is powered by Mercury Magnetics transformers that pump out through 2x12" Eminence speakers. It even has a switchable power attenuator, so you can lower output and still

get the output tubes to crank. Even my man George Benson has his own signature amp from Fender, which gives him enough headroom not to distort for his clean solos. They gave him three channels, of course all tube and a 1x12" Jenson speaker. I know George loves his Fender amps, and I've seen him use Fender Twins before to produce those smooth licks. In fact, long ago I opened up for Benson and Kenny G at Jones Beach Amphitheatre, and I used a Twin with a Marshall, as I mentioned earlier, and George was also using a Fender Twin.

Fender EVH 5150III 50-Watt Head piggy backed on 1970s Marshall Plexi Modded. That's what I'm talking about!

Fender has even moved into the twenty-first century with its new product, the Mustang. What is a Mustang? Well, I drive one, but for Fender it is basically a modeling amp designed like a combo with 1x12" or 2x12" Celestion speakers. You get a Twin, Deluxe, Bassman sounds with different effects and so forth. You can connect to your computer via USB through what is called Fender FUSE, which is software that enables you to record, edit, store, and share your music. Fender also has a new series for the bass player called the Rumble amps. I tried these recently, and they sound great and have easy and effective

Fender Eddie Van Halen 5150III 50-Watt Amp, three channels of shear tone, plus a bass resonance knob on the back plate!

Fender Pro Sonic Combo, which features 2x12"
Celestion sixty-watt speakers

controls to shape the bass for various tones. They come in different wattage models, but all are very compact, lightweight, and have that classic silver grill material. The controls, like days of old, are on the top of the amp and consist of an overdrive circuit with a three-button voicing section (bright, contour, vintage). Also included are an XLR line output, aux in, headphone jack, and an effects loop. It packs quite a punch, and depending on the voicing chosen, it takes you from vintage honky-tonk bass to shear metal mania tones and everything in between. It's solid state; however, I've always preferred solid-state amps for bass, because tubes get too mushy for the low frequencies. That's why metal guys like Dimebag Darrell used solid-state Randall amps because of their detuning. The low end of the guitar gets lost, but the transistors act in a different way and keep those frequencies tight. Look at the guitarist Fredrik Thordendal from the band Meshuggah; he uses the Axe-Fx II XL from a company called Fractal Audio. It's a digital modeling box, sort of an all-in-one amp/effects processor. It supplies a large number of virtual vintage and modern guitar amps, speaker cabinets, guitar stomp boxes, and multi-effects.

Fender Excelsior, part of the Pawn Shop Series powered by two 6V6 output tubes and two-12AX7 pre-amp tubes

Fender Excelsior back view, revealing the inner workings of the amp including transformers

Yes, Fender has jumped in the digital modeling arena full force. It even makes what it calls an Acoustasonic amplifier. It basically consists of various voicing controls to simulate sounds from an array of acoustic guitar types and electric guitar amps. It even features dual instrument/mic channels with independent EQ and effects controls. So you singer-songwriters out there can go play your favorite coffee house, plug a microphone into the amp, and play the guitar, thus becoming your own soundman with this one unit. Bring your electric guitar too, because the Acoustasonic features modeling Fender classic amps such as the blackface and tweed. It even offers settings to include British-style amp tones as well. On top of that it offers reverb, delay, chorus, Vibratone, and other effects that can polish up your shows. The amp also has what Fender calls "String Dynamics" control. This tones down those harsh treble frequencies associated with strumming acoustic guitars through piezo-type pickups.

All in all Fender found a new place in the market when it opened up the Fender Custom Shop and started building its Artist Signature Series, featuring players like Jeff Beck, Eric Clapton, James Burton, Steve Ray Vaughan, Will Ray, Danny Gatton, and of course Jimi Hendrix. Then it started reissuing all of its old amps like the Twin, Deluxe, and Super Reverb in the nineties. Hence, Fender is still with us and has had a long, sordid history, but has managed to remain a dominant force in the industry, while acquiring many other manufacturers that were once its rivals like Sunn Amps, Charval, Jackson, Guild, Gretsch, and even Kaman Music Corp, which owns Ovation and Hamer.

Fender Ramparte, another Pawn Shop Series amp, with nine watts of tube power, featuring "Hot & Cool" input channels

The Fender Vaporizer unleashes twelve watts from a pair of EL84 tubes. The Jetsons come to mind!

1965 Fender Deluxe Reverb "Pink Paisley." Buy the Fender paisley Tele resissue, and you're all set!

CHAPTER 3

British Invasion

Vox

This is a story that begins with the friendship of two World War II veterans, Tom Jennings and Dick Denney. They partnered up in the fifties to produce the AC15 amp that used the EL84 power tubes, commonly used in Britain. Jennings owned a music store called the Jennings Organ Company and sold the popular Univox electronic keyboard. Big band guitarist Dick was an amplifier designer and presented a prototype of the AC15 to Jennings, and the rest was history. The company was renamed Jennings Musical Industries, better known as JMI. Top musicians of the day in London used the

The indelible Vox Logo, synonymous with the sixties British Invasion

The Vox AC30 Super Twin Reverb Top Boost is the jewel in the crown for the company!

AC15 like Vic Flick, who recorded his iconic guitar riff for the "James Bond Theme."

AC30

By 1959 Vox was under the gun to produce a more powerful amplifier, one to rival Fender's Twin. So out came the Vox AC30, which would shape the British music scene for the next two decades. The AC30 featured the "Top Boost" circuit, which Vox became famous for inventing. The amp also had Celestion blue speakers with alnico magnets, another first in design. To accommodate the larger power, Vox expanded the cabinet and added an additional speaker. So now they had their own version of the Fender Twin cranking out thirty watts, just dirtier sounding with two 12-inch Celestion speakers, four inputs, and, like the Twin, two channels, Normal and Vibrato. It worked well and became the new standard for British guitarists of the time. Still, I think I would go with the original.

You certainly can't talk about Vox without mentioning the super group of the time who were the poster children for the amp, The Beatles. Vox had an exclusive deal in place with the band to supply all of their back-line amplifiers for live shows. John Lennon used an AC15, George Harrison used an AC30 with top boost, and Paul McCartney used the T60 solid-state amp with separate twelve-inch and fifteen-inch speaker cabinets. As the Fab Four become more popular, they needed more powerful amps to overcome the screams of the wild teenagers. So JMI gave George and John AC50 amps, which were piggyback units (separate amp head and cabinet). Paul was treated in using the powerful Vox AC100 head and T100 cabinet, which was comprised of 2x15" speakers. To keep up with Paul both John and George received their own AC100 amp heads with cabinets comprised of 4x12" speakers and two-horns. George moved on

Vox AC30 Super Twin Reverb Top Boost Vox controls, a real powerhouse for the early sixties

to the Vox 730 model with a 2x12" cabinet, which he used on recordings such as Revolver.

Star Power

But of course, the Beatles were not the only English band to use Vox. There was an army of successful Brit musicians in the sixties who used Vox, such as the Rolling Stones, the Yardbirds, the Kinks, the Who, and Thin Lizzy. The first American band to use Vox is noted as being the Brothers Grim in the sixties. Later US bands that used the Vox amps were the Monkees, Tom Petty, R.E.M., and Mars Volta. But one of my favorite guitarists, Brian May of Queen, immortalized the AC30. Brian was able to get the best tone out of the AC30 I ever heard; it's that hand theory again! Brian actually had a homemade treble booster built into his guitar. The Vox AC30 top boost feature originally came as a circuit board to install after the amplifier left the factory. The boost circuit had to be added to the back panel of the amplifier, with an additional tube mounted onboard. Later AC30s had the circuit built in from the factory with EQ controls on the top panel.

By 1960, Vox became an instrument dealer as well with five new guitars in its lineup: the Ace, Duotone, Soloist, Clubman, and Stroller, along with a three-pickup Consort and a two-pickup Escort. Vox also produced two bass guitars that year, The Contour and Bassmaster. However, they were outsourced and not manufactured by Vox but by Stuart Darkins and Co., a known furniture maker of the time. However, by the early sixties Vox came up with a design that would signify the change that was going on in that decade, The Phantom. It looked similar to a lute and was built from the ground up by Vox in its factory. Who could forget Rolling Stones guitarist Brian Jones playing a Phantom on the Ed Sullivan Show in the mid-sixties? Vox has reincarnated the Phantom in its new model the Apache, with similar shape and design.

Jim Marshall

The Marshall JTM 45 Reissue sounds as good today as it did fifty years ago.

When they say the mother of amplifiers is the Fender Bassman, it's not a joke. Here is a tale of another amp designer who took the Fender Bassman and reworked it for the new era with components he had on hand. The story begins with the birth of James Charles Marshall on July 29, 1923, in the damp English town of North Kensington. At the tender age of five, James was faced with great adversity when he was diagnosed

with what was called tubercular bones. This basically meant that his bones were very fragile and susceptible to easy breakage if he was not careful. It was a very Victorian type of diagnosis, which left him for years in a body cast trapped in an orthopedics hospital for much of his childhood.

Finally he was released from the hospital at thirteen years of age, to a world that was suffering from the Great Depression. Jim never went back to school; instead, he worked with his father in a restaurant to help the family survive. Jim had a remarkable reverence for working and desire to constantly move financially upward. In the book by Rich Maloof, *Jim Marshall, the Father of Loud: The Story of the Man Behind the World's Most Famous Guitar Amplifiers,* Marshall is quoted as saying,

> In my mind I thought, "I'm not going to be like my father." Because my father was always out of work, you see. This was 1937, and it was difficult for him to get a job. I thought, "I'm not going to be like that." So I worked as soon as I could. Then in the mornings at four o'clock I was filling milk bottles for Idris Jones, who did all the milk for around that area, and I was working at a jam factory during the day.

This was a very common feeling with this generation; the depression was not only financially debilitating, but also psychologically scarring. I could relate, because my father was born in Concord, Massachusetts, the same year as Jim Marshall, and that desperate financial anxiety experienced from the Depression stayed with him until the day he died in 2002.

Early Days

Jim was noted in having stage talent and was known to do performances in theatre and musical engagements. He had what was known as a crooner's voice, much like the late Rudy Vallée or Dick Powell. He was a tap dancer and all-around showman of the stage. Immediately what comes to mind is the classic film with Laurence Olivier called *The Entertainer* from 1960. Director Tony Richardson tells the story of the ill-fated Archie Rice, who is a down-and-out stage performer. It takes place in London with Rice trying to keep his career going as the music-hall tradition is fading from popular favor. However, in Marshall's world, big band and vaudeville were still very popular in Britain.

The world would change drastically from 1940 onward, for Europe ushered in an entirely new era. At seventeen years old, Jim tried to enlist in the Royal military service, but because of his childhood condition, he was not accepted. Instead, Jim worked as an engineer for both Cramic Engineering and Heston Aircraft through the war as he continued entertaining in the evenings. After the drummer was drafted from the band he was performing in, Jim jumped right in to take over on the drums. So now during wartime England, Jim was an engineer by day, and dragging his drums around London by night. Jim became the Phil Collins of his day both singing and drumming at the same time.

When 1945 came and the war ended, Jim found himself tinkering with electrical PA systems. He modded the PA his band was using, so he could hear himself singing while banging away at the drums. In turn, he made two custom speaker towers and left off the backs, making it easier to hear himself, because he always sat behind the PA when playing the drums. Hence the first open-backed Marshall was produced, a forecast for things to come. By the fifties Jim had become quite industrious, teaching drums to many aspiring students. In fact, Jim is noted as being the first to teach rock 'n' roll drum technique in post-war Britain. Some of his students, like Mitch Mitchell (Jimi Hendrix) and Mickey Waller (Small Faces, Jimmy Page, Jeff Beck), went on to play in famous rock groups. Jim also had secured an endorsement from Premier Drums. He received a small discount off of the drums when he purchased them directly from Premier.

JTM 45

The next logical step for Jim was to open up his own music store in 1960, called Jim Marshall & Son. His teenage son Terry worked in the shop while Jim gave lessons to his army of students. Marshall's ingenuity really blossomed when the store was opened and he started making custom speaker cabinets for guitar, bass, and PA systems. A very young Pete Townsend from The Who and Ritchie Blackmore from Deep Purple also goaded him into selling other instruments for their bandmates to buy. During this time the general public and music retailers didn't respect rock musicians, or the music for that matter. You see, Jim was teaching all of these kids drums, and those kids had young bandmates who wanted to buy instruments. Knowing a good thing when he saw it, Marshall naturally started to stock a variety of instruments. Remember this was the very early sixties and rock 'n' roll only existed in America; the Brits were still practicing for the invasion. In turn Jim was selling the Brit youths equipment, because he had the foresight to see that rock would take off in the UK as well. Boy was he ever right!

By 1962 Pete Townsend was wearing Marshall down to produce an amplifier that would blow people out of their seats. The consensus was that the Fender Bassman was close, but no cigar. Townsend wanted loud, louder, and loudest with dirty crunch. Finally when Jim agreed to make the amplifier, he recruited his in-house repairman Ken Bran and amp designer Dudley Craven. Together they took the basic design of the Bassman as a template and redesigned certain circuits. Replacing the Fender's 12AY7 pre-amp stage tube with 12AX7 value gave the amp more biting gain. Fender also changed the transformers and used output tubes 5881, which were military-grade 6L6s, and then switched to KT66s. These were surplus components and tubes that were available in 1962 England. It was the design's sixth prototype that won over Pete Townsend, when after he played it, he screamed, "That's it! That's going to be the Marshall sound from now on."

So this new Frankenstein amp was named the JTM 45, standing for Jim and Terry Marshall forty-five watts. Don't let the wattage fool you, they are super loud, and you need an attenuator or thirty acres of space to open it up to get that perfect tone of output-tube distortion. It was Ken and Dudley who electronically made the amp, but it was the sound Jim heard in his head that was put there by Pete Townsend. What a wonderful time to have been alive and to have seen this all go down and become a reality. It started slowly, making two per week, but by 1964 Jim's factory was making

twenty per week. And with the Who as his main client, Jim needed a factory just to produce enough for the Who's constant scrimmages onstage. Then came the design of the slanted 4x12" cabinet that housed four Celestion G12s, which Jim preferred over the straight cab design. The whole package was made, the hefty cabinet with the powerhouse head; what rocker would not be happy?

The Marshall JTM 45 had the most gain from any manufactured amp up to that time. A lot of it had to do with that nasty little 12AX7 tube that Ken and Dudley installed to replace the Bassman's 12AY7 tube. This was the missing link for amps, because the 12AX7 had a fuller overdrive tone for guitar. In actuality Leo Fender used the 12AY7 in the Bassman because he was catering to then-popular American Country music, which was the basis of his clientele. Ken and Dudley also employed some other subtle difference in capacitors, transformer power, output impedance, and a host of other electronic-component tweaking. But an important factor is also the use of those lovely Celestion speakers that love to break up tonally.

Marshall JTM 45 Reissue, the first amplifier designed by Ken Bran and Dudley Craven

Marshall JTM 45 Reissue: jump those two-channel inputs and get even more gain. Also pictured is the 100-watt JCM 2000 Dual Super Lead.

Iconic Guitarists

Another soon-to-be-famous guitarist frequented Marshall's shop, and that was Eric Clapton. Ah yes, you know where this is going. He wanted the JTM 45 in a combo version, because the 4x12" cab and separate head wouldn't fit in his car when he went to gigs. So instinctually Jim went ahead and built one for him, and Eric went on to make history with the amp in 1966 with John Mayall. He played those unbelievable solos on the *Blues Breakers* (a.k.a. *Beano*) record, like "Steppin' Out" and "Hideaway" with a Gibson Les Paul! There you have it: a match made in heaven, the Les Paul and Marshall! So where do you go from here? Well, at the demand of Pete Townsend—MORE VOLUME! So Jim built a 100-watt amp with an 8x12" cabinet; yes, you heard that right, one cabinet with eight 12-inch Celestion speakers in it. That soon was cut down to two cabinets with four 12-inch speakers because of the weight. Now you had that awesome backdrop onstage with the stacked Marshalls; this is what made rock 'n' roll!

There is another iconic guitarist who cannot go unmentioned when speaking about Marshall amps, and that's the one and only Jimi Hendrix. Mitch Mitchell, having been Marshall's top

drum students, took Jimi to meet Marshall one day. Hendrix wound up buying three complete Marshall full stacks and toured with them all over the world. Hendrix became the walking endorsement for Marshall; even to this day you see old pictures of Jimi onstage with stacks of Marshalls behind him. There is no better endorsement a manufacturer could ask for than the actual iconic figure with its equipment. The same could be said for Fender Stratocasters in the hands of Jimi Hendrix. A lot has been said about a Les Paul through a Marshall, but the same could be said for a Strat through a Marshall, as Hendrix proved. The 1967 release of *Are You Experienced* is certified proof of the Marshall power when coupled with a Fender guitar. We used to listen to it for hours, wondering how in the world Jimi was getting those sounds. Then came *Axis: Bold As Love*, which blew us away even further. It goes without saying that Hendrix was unbelievably talented, but those Marshalls made what he was hearing in his head a reality. And for us the immediate impulse was to run out and get a Marshall, at any cost.

Jeff Beck was ahead of the curve, using a fifty-watt Marshall with the Yardbirds and on his groundbreaking solo record *Truth*. When Beck left the Yardbirds, Jimmy Page reformed the band into the New Yardbirds, which turned into Led Zeppelin. After the first Zep album, the Supro wasn't cutting it anymore for Jimmy Page, so he went out and got himself a Marshall and a Les Paul and recorded "Heartbreaker," the quintessential guitar solo of the day. The tone of that amp with the Les Paul—man, what a fantastic combination! And don't forget those 200-watt Marshalls seen on Deep Purple stages through the early seventies screaming Ritchie Blackmore guitar riffs. And, of course, the pinnacle of all Marshall tone, Van Halen's first album featuring the guitar solo "Eruption." This was tone and playing that had not been recorded or

Marshall Plexi 100-watt model 1959 Super Lead, Damn Loud, but tone for days!

heard before Van Halen, changing the guitar world forever. In 1978 we all staggered back and were bewildered by how anyone could get such an out-of-this-world tone. Couple that with the two-hand tapping; it was unbelievable. That modded Marshall Plexi is the sound of shear tone heaven! I have a modded Marshall Plexi with a Mark Cameron mod adding an extra gain stage and a bass-resonance knob on the rear panel, which enhances the bottom end dramatically.

The Plexi

In 1966, Marshall model 1987 debuted featuring fifty watts of high-output gain. This amp differs from the JTM 45 in having deeper bottom response and a sharper pre-amp gain section, which gives it a fuller sound. By this point Ken Dudley had access

to better components and a higher grade of material. Plus remember Marshall had a huge success with the JTM 45 and saw what the new generation of players liked and what they needed more from the amp. This is when Marshall switched to EL34s for the output tubes and when, in my opinion, the amps started to sound like real Marshalls, not just modded Fenders. The transformer changed, and Marshall moved from a tube rectifier to a solid-state one. Through the sixties there was an uncertainty of the name of this amp, first called the JTM50, then JTM MKII, and then finally called JMP, standing for Jim Marshall Products. This is also known as Plexi's, named after the plexiglass front panels used at the time. With each incarnation, the gain section was tweaked to have more overdrive. Then came its big brother, the 1959 100-watt Super Lead; this is the one I have that is modded. This is directly related to Townsend's desire to have a 100-watt head for the internal volume war for the Who. This is also the amp that is seen stacked a mile high with Hendrix in the foreground.

By the mid-seventies came the design of the master volume for Marshalls in the 2203 model. Not everyone was playing arenas, so to maintain the desired Marshall overdrive tone for smaller venues, a new circuitry had to be designed. This would allow the guitarists to overdrive the pre-amp's tubes, not the output tubes, to get more gain. Two volume controls were designed, one for the actual pre-amp gain and the other for the overall gain of the amp. These amps were hugely successful and became a guitarist's best friend. It took the sound of the 1959 and modified it into an amp that could be played in lower-volume settings. It's very interesting, because Marshall was always listening to his customers and delivering what they needed. Since the first Marshalls, guitarists have always desired more gain, that's why overdrive pedals were made. But Jim was always trying to stay ahead of

Marshall Plexi 100-watt model 1959 Super Lead, with Mark Cameron mod, heavy duty baby!

the curve, adding more overdrive and power with each new model.

JCM Series

Then in 1981 came the hallmark JCM series, Jim's initials for James Charles Marshall. The first was the JCM 800, which took the eighties by storm, featured in every metal band's video. Besides the change of cosmetic nuances the new series had, the 800 had a more focused gain structure for modern guitar players. All of a sudden the old Plexi Marshalls were put out to pasture or had modification done to achieve more high-gain tone. The US models had a more mid-range bite to them, because many came equipped with 6550 power tubes, instead of the classic EL34 tubes. Even today metal heads love that amp for it's aggressive mid-range tone. On top of that, it featured channel switching from clean to

gain. Although the clean sound always sounded bad on these amps, it still gave players more options. It also featured effects loops to add even more value to the amp. Ironically these were all modifications people were doing to their previous Marshalls; Jim was just giving them what they wanted: more gain, two channels, effects loop, etc.

It got to the point that guitarists' ever-demanding desire for more gain surpassed what the JCM 800 had to offer. So the next step in gain evolution was the Marshall JCM 900, basically a JCM 800 modded pre-amp stage right from the factory. Like the 800s, they came as dual channels in fifty- and 100-watt versions, and as smaller combos. They featured a high and low switch to control the output power from pentode to triode operation. This controlled the output tube's elements, either running five or three elements, hence changing the tone of the amp. Unfortunately the 900s were not nearly as popular as the 800 series and don't have nearly as much value today. By the early nineties there were terrific Marshall-modded companies like Soldano that offered incredible-sounding amps that were really Marshall mods. So when the JCM 900 was released in the early nineties it had mixed reviews. That being said, my JCM 900 is a complete tone machine and has much more gain than the JCM 800. I think if Marshall had released them in the eighties, they would have really taken off; timing is everything.

Staying in the fashion of Marshall, Jim released the next stage with more gain called the JCM 2000 in the late nineties. It was marked with an additional moniker DSL, standing for Dual Super Lead. This also consisted of two channels, the first being Classic Gain that consisted of Clean and Crunch. They were going for the vintage Plexi tone, which unfortunately didn't hit the mark. The second channel, called Ultra Gain and consisting of Lead 1 & 2, was where this amp soared. This is in the fashion of a modded JCM 900; however, it

Marshall JCM 900 early nineties model sounds like a JCM 800 on steroids!

Marshall JCM 800 early eighties model with early seventies 4x12" speaker cabinet and Marshall Power Brake

Marshall JCM 900 view into the machine, simple like a 1965 Chevy, but extremely effective as a tone machine!

contained a Deep button that would scoop out the mid-range frequencies and add a bottom-end tone. There was a Tone Shift button that consisted of the controls Presence, Treble, Middle, and Bass to carve out your desired tone. Marshall then released the TSL series, Triple Super Leads featuring Clean, Crunch, and Lead channels. This is where the amp's

Marshall JCM 2000 Dual Super Lead: 100 watts of unadulterated GAIN!

overdrive started to sound transistor. They had a new feature called VPR that stands for Virtual Power Reduction. Basically it's an emulation button that can make the amp sound like a lower-wattage amp, which was not the most convincing but served the purpose of selling more amps.

New Era

When the term amp modeling is mentioned, one thinks of companies like Line 6. However, Marshall was the first amp company to explore the idea of modeling delivered in a compact size with the JMP-1. Designed in a one-rack space that was tube driven, it offered a plethora of Marshall sounds through history. This is a very useful studio tool for those who don't have access to Plexis, JMPs, JCMs, etc. Released in the early nineties, it's a digital unit that contained 12AX7 pre-amp tubes and four channels: two cleans and two overdrives. Typical of similar digital units of the time, the JMP-1s consisted of 100 patch points with which users could save their favorite patches. The rear panel had the following connections: Mains, Midi In/Thru/Out, Footswitch, Effects, send and stereo returns with level attenuator, master stereo outs L and R with level attenuator, and speaker emulator outs L and R with level attenuator.

The turn of the twenty-first century marked a new era for Marshall as it proceeded to look toward new territory. Hence you have the Mode Four, ranging in tones from the classic Plexi to the MESA/Boogie territory of low-end Metallica. Four amps in one, Clean, Crunch, Overdrive 1, and Overdrive 2, plus a three-way tonal switch for different high-gain sounds. This 350-watt amp also came complete with a tuner mute switch, two emulation-line outputs, and a built-in digital reverb. Because of the high output range of this amp, Marshall had to design an entire series of speaker cabinets to withstand the punishing sound. From the book by Rich Maloof, *Jim Marshall - The Father of Loud: The Story of the Man Behind the World's Most Famous Guitar Amplifiers*, Marshall reportedly carried a large bag of customer letters to his engineering department and told them, "Do what they want." Jim was a smart businessman; he never lost sight of his customers' needs. I mean, who was buying these amps in the first place? Rock stars? No, it was the average guitarists out there keeping manufacturers like Marshall in business. Just like he saw the desire for more gain in designing his earlier models, he was in touch with new guitar players. He knew the needs for high-gain amps that modern seven- and eight-string players wanted for their music.

Also a huge market for Marshall in the modern days has been reissuing its vintage amps, starting

Marshall JCM 2000 Dual Super Lead 401 in combo form

in the late nineties to present day. The first to come out of the reissue gate was the venerable JCM800 model 2203. There has been some debate on which JCM 800 model sounded the best, the one with

Marshall Micro stack miked with an SE VR1 Voodoo ribbon mic: try it! It sounds surprisingly good!

the two inputs side by side, which was an earlier version of the one with the inputs on top of each other. I've owned both models, and I have to say the later version with the inputs on top of each other sounds the best for lead-guitar tone. Also reissued at this time were the 2203 and, of course, both Plexi models: the 100-watt 1959SLP and the fifty-watt 1987X. The cool thing is that Marshall added the effects loop circuit into the Plexis, which was not available originally. Then a few years later in the early 2000s, Marshall reissued the JTM 45 and its 2x12" speaker combo renamed The Bluesbreaker.

Conclusion

They say imitation is the greatest form of flattery, and that stands true when it comes to Marshall amplifiers. Companies like Hiwatt, Laney, Blackstar, and the like have cloned Marshall's designs for years. Why? Well, because they sound so damn good. Where is there to go from the Marshall true gain tone? You certainly can modify an amp, but you are still covering the territory that Marshall has already treaded. MESA/Boogie did a great job of creating their distinctive tone as well. Again Randy Smith modified a Fender amp, this time a Princeton, creating a super-saturated gain tone, different from Marshall. But Marshall is distinctively its own monster and can't be duplicated. It's as British as the Spitfire plane from World War II and as aggressive as punk music from the grim streets of London, a perfect marriage between post-war British and American teenagers that created the greatest generational music ever heard.

This is my memory of my first Marshall that has stayed with me for decades. I was nineteen and answered an advertisement in the back of the Village Voice for a half-stack Marshall fifty-watt JMP series. I took the subway from my parents' NYC apartment on 85th street and Lexington Ave all the way down to the East Village. I walked into this small recording studio with the Marshall half stack set up. What a beauty! I played it and fell in love, wonderful tone and man it looked like the real deal. It even came with its own flight case for the 4x12" cabinet and the separate head. After I paid the guy, I rolled it out on the street and hailed the first big cab I could find. Those cabs are long gone from NYC, but they were fat-shaped checker yellow cabs that had a huge backseat with two folding jumper seats on the floor. I was able to fit the whole deal into the back. I remember getting back to the apartment and rolling the huge anvil cases into the lobby, where everyone knew me. Bobby the doorman was like, "Hey Buddy, what'cha got there, need help?" I wanted to get through the lobby quick in fear of seeing the super; then I would be in trouble. See, I wasn't the quietest guy in the world, and I didn't want to explain what I was doing. So I replied, "No, Bobby, I got it thanks!" I made a quick dash to the elevator and up to the sixth floor. I rang the doorbell, and my dad opened the door and saw me roll the anvil monstrosity into the foyer. Man, the look on the old guy's face was priceless. He said, "What in the world are you doing?" I said, "Oh, nothing, just got a new amp, don't worry it just looks louder than it is." There began my journey with Marshall amps; I still have that cabinet, seen in this book.

Marshall JVM 205H takes you from the JTM 45 to the JCM series, high gain!

Marshall Plexi and JTM 45, plus friends—No one said they would reproduce when I started out with one!

CHAPTER 4

DR. Z: Rise of a Boutique Builder

In the Beginning

Like many baby boomers, for Michael Dominic Zaite (a.k.a. Dr. Z), the 1960s played a huge roll in shaping his destiny designing amplifiers. Because his dad was a TV repairman, the family basement was full of tubes and test equipment. This of course was a natural place for a teenage boy and his band to rehearse and experiment with tube amps. Dr. Z recalls, "I would swap tubes, tweak biases and swap speakers. It whet my appetite for electronics, and that was a harbinger of things to come." Dr. Z went on to get an engineering degree, which led him to work in medical electronics for GE for fifteen years. Much of the seventies and eighties were spent in college,

working, and growing a family. By the end of the eighties, he went back to his first love of repairing tube amps. As he remembers, "Guys would bring me old Marshalls and Fenders, mostly for re-tubes and bias adjustments. The more I worked on these classics, the more I thought I could build an amp as good or better than these. That's what started me to build my own amps."

Dr. Z used Vox amps as a template for his first amp designs. He goes on to explain:

I often use the phrase, "The Holy Trinity Of Tone" in reference to Vox, Marshall, and Fender vintage-amp tones. I like to sprinkle a little bit

Dr. Z Antidote, powered by a matched pair of KT66 power tubes and equipped with an EQ bypass footswitch for sheer gain!

of all three in my designs if I can. I can recall taking the bus to downtown Cleveland to go to the Higbee department store, so I could just stare at the Vox amps. To me they were mesmerizing monoliths of sacred guitar tone and a joy to gaze at. I guess my first original designs used EL 84 tubes emulating the Vox sound.

Fender's Benchmark

I had to ask if the Fender Bassman is the blueprint or the mother ship for all amp designers, because so many noted amps like Marshall and MESA/Boogie started from the Bassman design. Mike stated emphatically:

Yes and no. When someone says a Bassman circuit, they are referring to an amp with a cathode follower that drives the tone stack. That's basically how the Marshall front end is, that's how Fender built amps in their tweed days, and the Voxes are the same way. It does have a unique sound to it. They went away from

that with the Blackface, where you go right into the tone stack from the gain stage, and then you recover it in the recovery stage. So there's a little bit of difference. With a cathode follower driving the tone stack, it drives a very big signal into your pots. What you are doing is taking away or sculpting away treble, middle, or bass with your tone knobs. When you have an amp like a Blackface design, you're adding frequencies because you have a recovery stage. Your signal is tiny to your pots. You're turning things up to add more frequency with your tone knobs, but with a cathode follower, you're taking frequencies away. The Bassman was kind of the mother of all. Then there are deviations from that, like when Ampeg used a back-stall tone stack; that's a little different. Probably 80 percent of recording from the sixties and seventies were played from the Fender Bassman front-end design. Later designers deviated by

Dr. Z's Remedy offers the classic Plexi tone. No need to jump inputs here; it's already internally wired for the crunch tone!

Dr. Z Carmen Ghia is powered by two EL84s' clean, crystal notes to smooth sustain in 18 watts. What more do you need?

using different output tubes, using different biasing circuits, added reverb or tremolo, or adding channel switching or boosting. You have to integrate clean sound first, because you can always layer on distortion, but you can't add a pedal that will give you a clean, three-dimensional sound.

Tube Technology

Amplifier manufacturers have tried everything through the past sixty years, starting with tubes, then going to solid state, now digital. But the truth is the original tube technology still sounds the best for guitar amps, a sound that cannot be emulated no matter how many amp farms you buy for the computer! Mike remembers thirty years ago when he started:

I wondered how long I was going to be able to buy tubes. Actually things have gotten

better; there are more and more Sovtek, New Sensor stuff, and JJ tubes being released. Newer and better and revised versions, like the KT66s and 88s, a lot of these tubes kind of went by the wayside, but they are now bringing them back. So there is more availability than ever, and God, they're seven bucks; they're inexpensive. In my top-of-the-line amp, the Z Wreck, I use a rare tube called a 6M14N, which is basically a military-grade EL84 tube. And I'm able to buy these; I just got another 200 from the Ukraine two weeks ago. It's all Soviet salvage. They are extremely durable; they can run a 5,000 to 10,000–hour operation and are extremely quiet. If there were ever a nuclear explosion, God forbid, the EMF that would generate would scramble every chip out there. So any electronic component would get wiped, but a vacuum tube would come right back on as soon as you applied power to it. The US government, as well as the Russian government, still has critical systems that use vacuum tubes just because of that reason. So they are not going to completely go away, and that's why Russia still builds so many great tubes. The EF86 tube I use in many of my designs was made by Svetlana, and man, I'm able to buy them by the hundreds, and I don't know how long it's been since they have been out of production. The New Sensor stuff that Mike Mathews has made doesn't sound too bad, and they're pretty rugged. The 12AX7 is a wonderful little pre-amp tube, and that little Tungsol reissue that they did, that's a great-sounding little tube. You know JJ makes a very nice tube, and that's out of what used to be

Czechoslovakia. That was a great tube company and where Tesla was born. The Tesla plant was there, and JJ bought the tube portion of the plant. You know Tesla is a big company in Europe like GE; they make refrigerators, and they make everything in Eastern Europe. Their tubes are good: very rugged and nice sounding. They are a little on the mid-rangy side; most of their tubes are EL34's and EL84's.

Mike emphasized the importance of building amps to match the tubes that are available:

We dial our circuits for the responses of these tubes. And if you're not able to do that, you can't build. My good friend, may he rest in peace, Ken Fischer of Trainwreck Amps,

Dr. Z Route 66, a nod to the great Marshall JTM 45 amp and Guitar Player Editors Pick in 1999

had a hell of a time. He would build his amps using incredible Brimars and Sylvanias, these wonderful European spec tubes. But once he couldn't get them anymore, you would give him a pair of Sovteks, and he would say, "Oh God, they sound terrible. I can't make an amp with these." You have to adjust! To be a good chef, you have take what stuff is in your pantry and make a good dinner. I get, from time to time, the dudes who say they've owned an amp for twenty years, and they never changed the tubes, and your amp blew a tube in two years. Well I can't buy old RCA tubes. I wish I could, but I can't. These guys don't realize too that the amp is on 'til two o'clock in the morning, and they throw it in their truck and drive down the street. They are bouncing the amp in the back of the truck; this stuff is fragile, man, and you got to be a little more careful with it. Most guitarists are very protective and take care of their amps. But there are some that figure it should work just like an appliance and think the next time they go gig, it should be perfect. The good thing is that there are young kids hearing the true, warm vintage sound of the tube today. So it's going to be hard for them to plug into a solid-state amp, as their playing gets better. The other thing is the feel. Being a player, you're used to leaning into things. That touch, that dynamic, that's what makes a great player, which separates the men from the boys. That solid-state stuff and that digital stuff takes all of that away. When I was working with Amplitube, I said let's make a power supply that is a little saggy. The problem is that digital needs plus or minus five volts; it's got to be rock solid. And if it goes to a certain threshold between a zero and a one, it's not as forgiving. The

beauty of analog is you can really stretch the parameters of the usefulness of a tube, and once it's warming you can get all sorts of different flavors and tones out of it. It's kind of hard getting that out of a chip. The other thing that always makes me laugh is I've worked on amps pretty much all of my whole life, and I'll get two Voxes in here, and they won't sound anything like each other. Things drift and change with age, with different tubes that are in them. I'm a purist, and I really believe in tube technology.

Dr. Z's Z Wreck, the top-of-the-line amp, is built to withstand the punishment of the players and still deliver a sweet tone!

As far as the argument between solid-state and tube rectifiers, Mike adamantly said:

I'm a die-hard tube rectifier guy! The tube rectifiers sound the best when you softly filter them, but don't over filter the power supply. Then that gives you that sag; you get the initial attack when the note hits, and then it sags a little bit and swells back up. That's called soft filtering. When you over filter an amp, it becomes a little lifeless and hard. It's great for the chunky kind of stuff that guys like with metal music, when they use those seven- or eight-string guitars. (Don't tell him I use an eight-string.) To get that entire low end, you do need a lot of filtering, so you don't get any modulation, just a pure note. When I'm designing an amp, I'll go back to lower the value of the caps, just before the point of "Ghost Noting." If you don't filter enough, you get a little aliasing notes. I use the saggiest rectifiers, 5Y3s. I use them in the Carmen Ghia. A lot of my other amps use 5AR4s. I get the Chinese 5AR4s that are a little softer than the Sovtek 5AR4s. Manufacturers will make the same tubes, but they will sound a little different from each other. But there are other things that play into effect, and the big thing is the output transformer. If the impedance is at a specific point, you are going to get a certain transfer from the plate of the tube to the output tube to the speaker. By varying the impedance, you vary the sound of the amp. Like with the Marshall JTM 45, originally made with radio output transformers, Jim Marshall bought surplus parts from a company called Radio Spares. Actually the impedance of the transformers was too high, and that's why the original Bluesbreaker amp sounds so good: it has this great distortion because it's not correct. God bless his heart,

Eric Clapton plugged his Les Paul into it and cranked it all the way and got those wonderful recordings on the John Mayall records. Talk about John Mayall, Dr. Z amps have appeared on the last eight John Mayall records.

The Dr. Z EZG 50 is powered by two TUNG-SOL 6L6GC STR to catch the wave for the surf sound!

Analog vs. Digital

Though Dr. Z is a true analog soldier like myself, he has expanded into the digital realm with Line 6.

The thing about electronics is that as time goes on, they get faster and cheaper. And that is basically what the holdup is right now. You still have to take an analog signal from a guitar, you have to convert it from analog to digital, and then take back from a digital signal to an analog one that feeds a speaker. There's a little time delay, but as chips get faster and faster, that gets less and less. The dynamics in the touch become better. And I think it will become a little more widely accepted. Digital is for the guys at home recording; it certainly makes it so much easier. A couple of manufacturers have utilized me like Line 6; there is a Route 66 and a Carmen Ghia sample. I also have a licensing agreement with Amplitube, so I'm an officially certified amp

Dr. Z M12 (Blackout), powered by 2 EL84 Cathode Biased tubes and sharing the same tone-stare design as the Route 66

company with them. I sent them amps, we worked together a little bit, and they sampled the stuff and sent it back to me. It's pretty good for what it is. I've worked in high-tech medical electronics for fifteen years, and I've seen the leading-edge stuff. Yeah it's cool and all, but there is something alive about tube amps. It's living; it's breathing. It's air, and it's an instrument. There are intangibles that are

Dr. Z Maz8 boasts a pre-amp stage powered by four 12AX7 and one 12AT7, but at reasonable levels coming in at only eight watts!

just not there, like the power-supply sag, the touch dynamics, the swelling of the note, the air pressure in the room from the movement of the speaks; all that kind of stuff they really can't simulate, all of the millions of things we deal with on a daily basis. I look at the digital stuff as a tool, it's not bad, but there's still a long way to go. I believe as technology gets better it will be easier to integrate, like PCs, once memory chips became so inexpensive, the power of the PC became more and more.

You can obviously hear the difference in the new digital recordings on the radio, as Mike states:

I listen to digital recordings, and the stuff is so transient, so spiky, that it's fatiguing. After listening to it, I want to just turn it off; it's too perfect and dynamic. Man, your ears don't hear that way; your ears hear rhythmically. You want to have that little bit of analog. Look, I can listen to a tube stereo all day, twenty-four hours a day. It doesn't hurt, but man, the car radio, I've got to just reach over and turn it off after a while; it's just too much. Young people are finding that the old way is better. The older, they get, the more they realize the older unsophisticated sounds are always better. Maybe unsophisticated is the wrong way to say it; it just sounded more genuine.

Innovative Amps

I wanted to see how Mike gets his innovative ideas and creates new tone machines. Brian I have always taken a recording or something that catches my ear, and I think, "Oh man, that amp sounds great, what is that?" I'll try to research it or try to find one. I'm sixty-three, and I have weathered a lot of equipment. I can remember some of these amps that sounded so great. I just released an amp called the Therapy, and basically it is a low-powered tweed kind of sound. I don't just clone the amp; I don't just knock off the circuitry. I try and take that sound as a foundation and say, how can I do it using today's parts? I did some work on this, came up with a design, and emulated the sound pretty well. I have my own forum, and there was a guy on there who had a 1952 tweed twin and said, "I'll be the judge of how well you were able to duplicate that sound!" The guy made a recording, and it's amazing how similar they sound, even the guy couldn't believe it.

When I designed the Therapy, I found a guy who was hand rolling capacitors; his company is Jupiter Capacitors. I tried these caps, and they sounded so good. It hearkened the days when I first started with amps. I always loved music; I played when I was a kid. I'm in Cleveland, and there is a lot of rock 'n' roll, so I started fixing my friends' amps. Prior to building my own amps, I remember a friend of mine brought me a 1959 Bassman that he carried into my basement as if he was holding a newborn baby. It was so precious to him. It was humming like crazy, so I said let me figure out what's going on with it. So I found that a couple of Astron caps were leaking onto the output tubes. I changed all of the caps with orange drops. He came back to pick up his amp, plugged in, and started to cry saying, "What did you do to my amp, it sounds terrible? So I put back the old Astron caps and just replaced the ones that were bad. All of a sudden the amp sounded better, and he was happy. I took that as a life lesson. Just fix

what's broken, especially with vintage gear. I could never find those caps that were in that amp again, but this kid from Jupiter touted his caps sounded like those old Astron caps. Boy, they do sound good; I put them in the Therapy, and WOW!

Originally I thought the KT 45 amp was a nod to the old Marshall JTM 45, but it turned out to be

The Dr. Z KT 45 was originally designed as a kit amp, but prudent judgment ruled the day, and it became another design by Dr. Z using an EF-86 (pre-amp tube) in the front end.

a different story behind it. He told me:

Do you remember the early nineties? There there were a lot guys making amp kits, so that is where the KT 45 came from; I was going to make a kit. I remember talking with my attorney, and he goes, "I really think you shouldn't do that; you should really think about that. The liability you are going to have, some guy is going to electrocute himself and burn down his house. You are going to have a lot of phone calls, a lot of questions from people with various amounts of knowledge. He talked me out of it, so I kept the KT 45 name.

Dr. Z Maz 18 is the perfect small-venue amp, still with eighteen watts of punch and power!

Dr. Z Stang Ray was a collaboration between Brad Paisley and the Doctor to get that palette of tones.

Inner Electronics of the Beast

Voltage: Dr. Z warns us about being careful with electrical charges stored in amps, even when unplugged from the wall, because the capacitors hold electrical current.

If you don't discharge them, they'll hold that voltage, because they are basically little batteries. There are a couple hundred volts; it's a very low current. When people get electrocuted and really hurt themselves, it's generally from the shock; they fall down or get thrown against the wall. You've got to be careful. I worked with x-ray machines that had thousands of volts, amazingly high voltage, which is very, very deadly. I mean, I still get bit every once in a while. You have to have a healthy respect for it.

When dealing with various voltage currents from around the world, Mike explains:

You have to match the voltage coming out of the wall, and that does vary from country to country; you try and catch it all by doing a 235-voltage transformer. Where the problem comes in is in the frequency, the 50hz. You're getting closer to DC, a Direct Current, and then the lower you go. When you do that, you generate more heat, so that's what you have to watch out for. Generally speaking you have to use a little more expensive laminates. You have to use a M6 laminate when you design the transformer, so it will dissipate the heat much better, without having a huge transformer. The standard transformer is a M15, but when you start going into fifty hertz, and you want to keep it the same size, you just increase the quality of the laminate. As far as the voltage is concerned, you have to be careful when using small tubes like EL84s. The power transformer is a step-up transformer, where you're taking 100 volts from the wall, and you're stepping it up three times to make 300 volts on the plate of the tube. Voxes are typical of this kind of problem with EL84 power tubes. You can only put so many volts on the tubes, or they are going to red plate and fail. Tubes like the EL34 and 6L6 are used to handling 400 to 450 on their plates and probably won't break a sweat; fifteen to twenty volts one way or another won't really affect them. Little tubes like EL 84's are more sensitive.

I have a domestic and an export transformer, and some the trannies I install have dual primaries, so they can run 110 or 220 volts. What I found is that it is an expensive tranny when you have a dual primary. If I only do 10 to 15 percent of my business as export, it doesn't make sense to make them all dual primaries, because I'll only use one out of ten to go to export. Every penny counts when you are a manufacturer and build 1,500 to 2,000 amps a year, it does add up. So I have designated trannies for Europe. The biggest problem I have is Australia, because its wall voltage is close to 245. You certainly have to

have something specially designed to operate there. It's so expensive to export out there 200 to 300 hours added to the cost of the product just in shipping and the exchange rate of the dollar. It's not easy going through customs and all sorts of regulations.

I wanted to get a definitive answer on what exactly was impedance. Mike explains:

Well that's resistance that changes from frequency. So that's the whole beauty of a speaker. You hit a specific note, you have a specific frequency, and you're going to have a specific resistance that's going to attenuate that note. And to simulate a speaker's output, that's a pretty convoluted set of parameters to try and reproduce. Some of these guys are doing a pretty good job with these attenuators right now. They've got chokes, caps, and little transformers inside of these things to try and be a speaker emulator. The more they can do that, the more real and natural it sounds.

Dr. Z Mini Z especially for the apartment guitarist, a 5-watt amp with a built in attenuator.

Proof's in the Pudding

There is nothing like the compliments of an artist using your designs to make an amp designer feel pretty damn good! Mike recalls:

I went to see Steely Dan this year, and Walter Becker had six Dr. Z amps on stage. I brought him a new amp, a Therapy, and he used it that night at the show. I was amazed! For him to do that, I was like, "Oh my god!" You get to meet some of these amazing artists. It adds richness to your life. It separates the men from the boys. In the beginning of my career I met a guy named Charlie Jobe who worked for Hammond organ. He did percussive mods on

Dr. Z Monza driven by a post-phase inverter master volume and sixteen-ohm speaker output.

all of the B3s, and I spent many hours talking with him. Jimmy Smith was one of his big artists, and when Jimmy got a new organ, he would take it to Charlie's shop for mods. But there was one thing Charlie told me. He said when these guys want you, they will get hold of you for your services. Don't take advantage of knowing them, asking for tickets to a show; don't do that BS man. If they don't want you, they won't take your calls. I lived by that, and because of that, I've known so many artists that I work with, so I just take a step back. I know amp builders that are just nuts for that shit! They go to the shows, they want to go to the NAMM shows, they want to go to the award shows, bringing amps and giving them to guys. Dude, I'm sorry, but I don't have time for that. I mean, I belong to NAMM, but I've never shown. I couldn't afford going to LA with a truck full of amps and a soundproof room. Then you have to come back with twenty to thirty new dealers, or it's not going to be worth doing. I've got to look at it as a business thing, because you're spending all of this money. And for me I couldn't handle twenty to thirty new dealers. I kind of stay in my little niche and am happy. There are a lot of pedal companies that will call me up and ask me for an amp for their

Dr. Z Therapy: the good doctor orders some real tone therapy, so take your medicine!

booth, so there are Dr. Z amps at the show. There are too many people that infiltrate the NAMM show; they are not the professionals; it's not just for dealers anymore. It would be nice if Saturdays and Sundays would be open for the public, but Monday through Friday it's just for business. The Nashville Summer NAMM is more controlled, and people in Nashville aren't so starstruck.

UL Approved

Dr. Z knows that in today's market, a guitar amp has to be pretty damn good to get recognized. He states that what sets his amps apart is,

Our amps are UL certified, and to my knowledge we are the only boutique amp builder that has it's amps laboratory certified for safety and quality to UL 60065 standards. Our amps go through a rigorous test to assure the public the highest quality construction and safety standards are met. Being built like a tank is not just a catchphrase here; it is a tested, certified commitment to the highest quality. It's a difficult thing for a handmade tube amp with 1950s technology to be up to today's standards. I have a huge distributor in Canada, Long & McQuade; it has about fifty to sixty stores, so it's a big player. It had problems bringing in my amps, because I was not CSA approved, the Canadian safety standard. I had to become CSA for them to

Dr. Z's Z Wreck is a dual creation between Brad Paisley and the good doctor with thirty watts of sheer tone!

stock my amps on the shelves. It was a very costly thing, about $10,000 to $15,000 per amp to have them tested and approved. So four times a year, they send an inspector in here to make sure we are using the correct transformers, and we didn't change anything. I'm proud of the fact that I'm an engineer, and I designed this stuff, and it was correct. I cannot only say that, but I have a laboratory that passed it and said I did. Fender and Marshall, the big manufacturers, have to be UL approved, but they can absorb the cost of that. In Germany I have to pass the regulations, like I have to cage in the tubes, so a little kid can't put his finger in it. It's pretty much all safety-related stuff. I got the JET, the Japanese electronic testing, done on my amps, so I'm able to import into Japan.

The Future

Mike is working on some great new retro amp projects that will be perfect for the studio musician.

There are a couple of amps I'm working on, one is a Gibson model called the RTV79; it's a little stereo amp. It's got 2x10" speakers and two EL84

output tubes. There are two outputs, and there's a stereo jack in the center of it. It's an amazing amp and sounds like nothing else I've heard. Another one is the Gibson GA40, which is the Les Paul amp. Those things sound amazing; they are great-sounding little amps. Low wattage seems to be the way to go; who can play a 100-watt amp anymore? There is nothing like third and fifth harmonics from a power tube distorted. That's the life man! I've played with the variable voltage circuits to lower the voltage to the plate of the output tube; they are OK in a very small range. If you look at the data sheet for a power tube, you'll see the plot; you'll see the operating perimeters for that tube. You start getting beyond the bell curve of where that tube is supposed to operate; you're in no man's land. It might sound good or it might not.

Like any proud inventor and designer, I wanted to see what amp was the apple of Mike's eye.

Brian, they're like my kids. I've built thirty-two different models through the twenty-eight years I've done this, and the newest one, the Therapy,

Dr. Z's Z 28: no, not a fast car but a clean, sweet-sounding amp powered by two 6V6s

is one that I'm really, really proud of. The Route 66 was one the first I built and a tip of the hat to the Bluesbreaker. In 1999 the Route 66 got the Guitar Player Editors' Pick Award. It's such a unique-sounding amp; they started that award that year. The Guitar Player Editors really look toward new, original builders, not guys who just copy schematics from the Tube Amp Book by Aspen Pittman. The one thing about Fender is you can copy a design, without really knowing how to read a schematic. In Pittman's book, you'll see they'll have assembly drawings as well as schematics. The assembly drawings are where all of the caps and resistors are located; it's a typographical kind of drawing. So it became very easy; you didn't have to have electronics chops. Just a good ear, a good solder, and a desire to do it. But still to this day I plug into an amp I just built, and it's like giving birth, it's a cool thing!

Dr. Z's Maz 38, a combo used by Joe Walsh himself, features the foot-switchable EQ bypass, giving a great lead boost

Dr. Z's SRZ is a heavy amp with three 12AX7 cascaded gains in the front end and sixty watts of glorious crunch!

CHAPTER 5

The Players

A Seymour Duncan Convertible 100-watt head with built-in attenuator and exchangeable tubes, way ahead of its time

Jeff Beck

British producer-keyboardist Andy Wright produced one of my favorite Jeff Beck studio albums, *You Had It Coming.* I love the way the break beat sound meshes with Jeff's awesome, overdriven blues-rock licks, producing the driving, metallic sound. Naturally I was anxious to see how Jeff approached his tone and what amps he used for the sessions.

According to Andy, Jeff's techs arrived with a Marshall JCM 800 head, a 4x12" cabinet, Beck's signature Fender Stratocaster, and a Cry Baby wah pedal. They placed the amp and cabinet in the vocal booth of his programming room and placed a Shure 57 in front of the cabinet, about two inches from the middle. The mic connected into an Urei 1176 that connected into a Digidesign 888. Andy monitored twenty-four channels from Pro Tools through his Mackie SR32 mixer. The majority of the guitars were recorded in Wright's programming room. A very simple signal chain and process, but that's all you need when you're recording Jeff Beck!

Then came the magic from Jeff's hands; once he started to play, a plethora of sounds emerged from the JCM 800. A true master at work, starting from his hands, generating through the strings on the strat, and into the Marshall, no BS, just straightforward talent. As Andy explains, "He regularly did takes with the Cry Baby set to a static position, which sounded really edgy, and I had a habit of cranking the Mackie desk EQs until it sounded like it does on the record. We often joked that Jeff would sound amazing playing a cheap supermarket guitar, and to be honest, I would say that may not be too far from the truth!"

For some of the other tracks, Andy booked two weeks at Metropolis Studio A, which featured a Focusrite mixing console. They recorded Jeff's band in there, to get the ambience of the live room.

Jeff Beck painting by New Jersey artist Todd L.W. Doney

Expecting a huge number of amps and guitars, Wright was ready for the attack, but as he states, "When I turned up that morning, I saw Jeff's technician arriving in a car only to reposition the JCM 800, 4x12", and Strat in the vocal booth of Studio A. We recorded some valuable parts in those sessions." My favorite guitar tracks on the record, "Nadia," along with "Blackbird," were recorded in Studio A, and the live guitar sound was from the large ambience of the room, captured by a Brauner VM1 microphone. Andy said, "The cabinet also had a Schoeps M221 series mic directed at it. Jeff, however, seemed to prefer the intimate environment of the programming room. He positioned himself about a yard away from the glass door to the vocal booth, and as the soundproofing was not particularly good, he could partially hear the sound from the amp with the door closed."

Well done Jeff and Andy! The guitar tone on the album really growls without being obnoxious, but also delivers a warm tube tone. The Marshall JCM 800 is still a tone monster and is always a great bet for devastating guitar tone!

Zakk Wylde

Barking at the Moon—Zakk Wilde (Photo by Don Mitchell)

The Wylde Irish boy from New Jersey really showed the world he could take the guitar farther than any of his predecessors, and in the past two decades with Ozzy, as well as in his own solo projects, he has emerged as a major influence to metal guitarists everywhere.

Thinking back to the early eighties, I remember when Randy Rhoads played guitar for Ozzy and how in awe we all were of Randy's techniques on those two ground-breaking records, *Diary of a Madman* and *Blizzard of Ozz*. Followed up by the intense shredding of guitarist Jake E. Lee on *Bark at the Moon* and *The Ultimate Sin*. Zakk had some really big shoes to fill, but he proved himself to be worthy of the

task and then some. In 1992, when I saw Zakk at the Coconut Teaser in LA with his southern rock band, Pride and Glory, I was able to see what an amazing showman he was and hear his great vocal talents as well. I later picked up a Randy Coven album with the song, "I Wish" on it, and there was Zakk singing his heart out, sounding very much like Gregg Allman. Later, in the nineties, he formed the heavier-than-thou band, Black Label Society.

Zakk explains what he brings to the studio when he is recording his devastating tones. "For guitars, I'll bring the Les Paul and the Rock Replica Randy Rhoads polka dot V guitar made by GMW Guitar Works that I like to use on solos. I will also use a twelve-string and six-string acoustic—I bring the whole arsenal. I like to go through different amps to see what works, but I'll usually use just one. I'll bring the Marshall JMP, JCM800, and JCM2000, but usually use the 800. I will also bring a Roland JC-120 Jazz Chorus. You bring all your crayons with you; it's not like you're going to use all sixty-four of them, but if you need them, they're there."

Hal Lindes

My good friend Hal Lindes is perhaps best known as a member of the multi-platinum band Dire Straits. His distinctive sound and influence can be heard on such landmark albums as *Love Over Gold* and *Alchemy*. Having been privileged in working with Hal on several projects, I can say he is one of the most underrated guitarists. His true understanding of the guitar and all it holds in tone and passion is remarkable. He is always my first choice when choosing a guest guitarist and my first call man of the hour.

When approaching tone Hal generally starts out with either an early sixties cream Strat or one of his Schecter Strats through a 1984 Fender Concert RI (2x10"). For a different tone, he goes

Hal Lindes of Dire Straits, smiling for the paparazzi

Larry Carlton

Rolling Stone magazine listed Mr. 335 as having the tastiest guitar lick on the Steely Dan song, "Kid Charlemagne," and it is no wonder that he

Larry Carlton with his signature Gibson ES 335 guitar

for either the 1957 Fender Tweed Twin or his stage rig Boogie and Marshall 4x12" cab. Hal recalls that, "Fender provided a host of Concert amps to test out, resulting in the selection of a killer-sounding tone machine that really stood out from the pack. Mark Knopfler was also using that Concert initially while in the formative stages of shaping the tone for the 'Money For Nothing' riff."

When recording in the studio, the main microphones were mostly, "Neumann U67s, AKG 451s and Shure SM57s. The amps were miked with a SM57 on the speaker, a U67 slightly back, and one or two overhead mics to capture the room ambience." This was all recorded on a Sony 3324 Digital 24-track recorder. Like many other famous bands of the time, Dire Straits did additional recordings and mixing at The Power Station in New York. "The building was originally a Consolidated Edison power plant, then a sound studio where the television game show *Let's Make a Deal* was filmed, and by the early eighties became the Mecca of recording studios."

also has a long history with amps. Having played a great many amps in his life, Larry knows when an amp feels good and achieves "his" sound. Back on *Strikes Twice* he was still using his original MESA/ Boogie. It didn't have a name like Mark I or II then; it was just one of the first amps made. Larry later switched to Dumble amps in the eighties and has never looked back. He commented,

I've been playing Dumble for almost twenty-five years now. There is no comparison to the sound and approach to Mesas. I stopped using the Boogies around 1982. I had two, the original two I had purchased, and over the years the capacitors had dried up and had to be rebuilt. Randy Smith over at Boogie was wonderful to me. He went through all of my specs on my amp and built me another one trying to duplicate the originals, but they didn't quite sound as good as the originals. So when I discovered the Dumble, my tone went way up, the quality of the sound went way up, and I kind of noticed over the years the sound of Boogie was sounding very processed. And I didn't relate to that. So I have two Dumbles, one for stage and one for backup. The head is separate and the 1x12" speaker, cabinet Dumble designed to go with the head.

In 1971, when Larry was twenty-three years old, which was the beginning of his career, he started playing with Joe Sample in the Crusaders. He remembers,

The first week recording with the Crusaders, we did a cover version of Carol King's "So Far Away," and I was using the volume pedal through my amp making little crying notes, and it was real new back then; nobody was doing that. And they told me later after the recording that the producer and the engineer in the booth said to each other, "What the hell was that?" after they heard the crying guitar sounds. They hadn't heard anything like that or at least the way I did it. So yeah we kind of created a new sound early in the seventies. (Don't tell him that Hendrix and Clapton used a wah years before.)

Gary Hoey

Another good friend of mine is the incomparable Gary Hoey, who has an incredible collection of music releases. Hoey has a total of sixteen albums and five top-twenty Billboard hits and is listed in the top 100 greatest guitar players of all time. A lot of us remember his 1993 breakthrough remake of "Hocus Pocus" on Warner Bros Records, which landed him a top-five position on the Billboards charts. The Boston-raised guitarist followed up with the soundtrack to the surf saga, *Endless Summer II*. And of course,

Gary Hoey with his Fender "American Flag" Strat ready to ROCK!

who can forget his popular *Ho! Ho! Hoey* Christmas releases? Gary has played with the best of them: Brian May (Queen), Ted Nugent, Foreigner, Joe Satriani, The Doobie Brothers, Kenny Wayne Shepherd, Eric Johnson, Steve Vai, Peter Frampton, Rick Derringer, and Deep Purple.

Gary uses several amps in his arsenal. The main amp is the EVH 5150III, a great choice. "It's an amazing three-channel amp. Many people don't know how amazing it is. (Don't tell anyone.) I also used the Peavey Triple XXX, Diezel, and a Marshall." In recordings he would layer eight rhythm tracks together, creating a sonic landscape of heavy guitar rhythms. Gary told me, "One sound would be bassier, and one more mid-range, and when you combine it, it's huge. You have to play super tight and mix the levels carefully just sneaking in a tone."

Gary made a great study on the classics growing up, like myself, to choose the right amp and tone. Gary said, "So I would study *Blow by Blow* by Jeff and *Elegant Gypsy* by Al Di Meola. Then Joe Satriani, Steve Vai, and Eric Johnson showed that you could make it commercially viable." Producer Richie Zito taught Gary that when recording in the studio, always keep on hand many amps and guitars, because changing an amp for different tempos and keys can make all the difference.

Leslie West

Leslie West laying down guitar tracks at Jungle Room Studios

When I was producing/engineering Randy Coven's release, *Nu School*, the guest guitarist was Leslie West. For those of you who are not familiar with this guitar icon, West started his musical career in the sixties. In 1969, West and Pappalardi would form the pioneering rock band Mountain. Felix Pappalardi was the famed producer of Cream's groundbreaking album, *Disraeli Gears*. Mountain also graced the stage at the 1969 Woodstock; unfortunately, if you weren't at the show you never would have known it! At the time, West did not sign the release form by the film company, and therefore their live performance was lost in history. Confidentially, West told me that was the worst decision he ever made.

So in comes West and Coven, and I can tell from Randy's face he was nervous right off the bat. Straightaway I set West up with my Brown Tone modified 1983 Marshall JCM 800 and Ibanez 808 Tube Screamer. Leslie immediately turns every knob on the amp to ten. The amp cabinet was in an iso booth across the room, where I near miked the cabinet with a Beyer M160. West immediately started to bark orders and insisted the isolation room door be open, which I thought, "Well, that defeats the purpose," but went along with it. So I placed a Neumann TLM 149 about five feet back outside of the booth. West apparently wanted to feel the bottom boom of the cabinet, so the cabinet rang through the control room.

Soon into the session I realized why Randy was so nervous. West had never heard the songs before and was critical of everyone's parts. "Who the hell is the drummer? He's all over the place! More Delay! Less of the band! Get me a Diet Coke! Where the hell is Coven?" Well Randy had snuck out of the session to smoke half a pack of cigarettes; the poor guy was a nervous wreck. So I had to send someone out to get Randy back in the control to suffer equally like the rest of us. Plus Randy needed to guide Leslie through the song for direction, but that wasn't going to happen. So I just recorded everything, so I could go over it later to construct some sense out of it. Now I'd like to remind everyone I wasn't recording this digital with a flip of the space bar. No sir, I recorded this all on analog on an Ampex MM1200 two-inch, twenty-four-track machine. For those of you who are not familiar with it, there is a delay on the punch in and out on the machine, and it always sounds as if you cut off the punch in and out when monitoring. So I caught hell for that as well and had to remind West that it's fine when you play it back. Believe we all got gray hair that session.

Randy Coven

Another good friend, God rest his soul, Randy was a very underrated bass player. I worked with him a lot and produced, engineered, and played

Randy Coven recording his solo release, Nu School *at Jungle Room Studios*

guitar on his last release, *Nu School*. Randy had a very interesting background—he went to Berklee College of Music in Boston and was roommates with none other than Steve Vai. They were in several bands together back in the eighties, and in fact, Randy told me that he actually lent Steve Vai the money to make a phone call to Frank Zappa, which led to Steve getting the gig being Zappa's musical transcriber. Randy received a lot of acclaim back in the eighties from the magazine, *Guitar for the Practicing Musician*. The magazine had its own record label at the time, called Guitar Recordings, which released a lot of shredders, one being one of the best, Randy.

When I started recording Randy in the beginning, he had brought in a little Ashdown amp stack with ten-inch speakers, which really wasn't cutting it. So I took a direct signal into tape with a Radial box onto a separate channel and wound up mixing both the amp track and the direct track together. On the next session we moved right away to a Fender Bassman 100 with a fifteen-inch speaker. We started the session by placing the bass amp in the isolation booth. I miked it with an AKG D112, going to a channel on the Trident console. I always had great results getting Randy's tone from the Bassman; it has a built-in EQ feature, along with a compressor. Also, on the back, it has an XLR connection for direct recording as well as a volume pot for line-out levels. I found for recording purposes this amp did quite well with little fussing. I have had guys bring in huge tube bass amps with these huge cabinets, and they sound so muddy, with no definition, making it a chore to get a good tone from them. Best thing to do is think small for the studio and concentrate on good tone, not massive size for the amp.

Fender Bassman 100 amp, among friends in the isolation booth

CHAPTER 6

Amplifier Designers

amplifier designers amplifier designers
amplifier designers amplifier designers

Ampeg

Ampeg is one of America's amp icons. It all started with the man by the name of Charles Everett Hull from Wisconsin. A piano player turned bass player in the forties, he soon realized that the upright acoustic bass, much like its cousin, the guitar, at the time could not project its beautiful tone over the jazz bands of the day. So like every good inventor, Charles was on a mission to enhance the bass sound, and what better way to do it than to build his own pickups and amps. By the early fifties Hull had an amp-manufacturing store in New York. Being a real perfectionist, he hired a skilled

Family values in the Ampeg Family Portrait: no nudging or crying boys, just say cheese!

electrician by the name of Jess Oliver who went on to design many successful products for Ampeg.

At the time, its biggest competitor was Fender Amplifiers, which Hull hated for the amps' harsh mid-range tones. So Ampeg produced more HI-Fidelity amps that were very clean and full sounding like the early Jet 12-R, the Portaflex, and the Rocket. But it was not until the 1969 NAMM Show in Chicago that the design team unveiled the iconic bass amp SVT (Super Vacuum Tube) that sported fourteen tubes, six of which were huge 6146 power tubes. To accompany the tubes were gigantic transformers, which brought the weight close to 100 pounds for the amp head alone.

A classic if there ever was one: 1960 Ampeg M-15

Now ironically, to Hull's chagrin, the Rolling Stones made the SVT famous. According to Ampeg, in a panic, the then Stones keyboard player and road manager Ian Stewart contacted Ampeg's LA guy, Rich Mandella, desperately pleading for some free amps that the Stones could use on their upcoming tour that was just weeks away, which Mandella quickly provided, delivering a good number of the SVT prototypes and old 4x12" cabs to the Warner Brothers lot, where the Stones were rehearsing in an unused soundstage. Once Keith, Mick Taylor, and Bill Wyman plugged into the SVT prototypes, they where relentless. According

to Mandella, "Everything he (Keith) was doing in rehearsal just kept getting louder, bigger, and crazier, with two or three heads per person. I'd watch the amps, and when I could see one was about to explode, I'd just switch heads."

When the Stones departed for their tour that

What a great year for music! 1965 Ampeg Gemini I

year, Rich Mandella escorted them backstage as their personal Ampeg technician and kept a watchful eye on the SVT equipment and the temperamental blokes who bashed them.

Ampeg Product Manager Zane Williams explained his background and experience with the amp giant.

Ampeg is the world's first, largest, and most renowned bass amp company. Ampeg is not only the original bass amp company, it is also considered the gold standard for bass amplification worldwide today. Founded in 1949 by Everett Hull, a working stand-up bass player who sought to bring the acoustic stand-up bass to levels that equaled the massive sound of a full

The glow of the tubes and the heat of the amp: Ampeg Heritage B-15N

Big sounds do come in small packages: Ampeg GVT52-212

live jazz band. He replaced the "peg" that the stand-up bass would typically rest on with an "amplified peg," which had a microphone situated at the top, which would belly inside the stand-up bass and feed a signal to a small tube amp he created just for his bass. His wife later coined the name "Ampeg," stating he needed to come up with a cleverer name for his new product. From Hull's Amplified Peg, to Jess Oliver's famed B-15 flip-top (the most recorded amplifier in history) to the arena-rattling SVT stack created by Bill Hughes and Roger Cox in the late sixties, Ampeg has literally helped shape the sound of classic and modern music for the past sixty-six years. Ampeg was also the first company to put reverb in a guitar amplifier (not Fender) when the Reverberocket was first introduced in the early sixties and then reissued just a couple of years ago with the Heritage R-12R.

I was curious if Hull & Oliver were influenced by any amplifier designs for certain classic tones, but Zane adamantly said, no! He went on to explain,

As Ampeg is considered the originator, and it blazed the path for others to follow, many followers have since attempted to find the magic that exists in every Ampeg amplifier. It may be fairer to note that the founder of Ampeg started during a time where "clean" amplification was key. No distortion and accurate replication with as much headroom as possible were the goals. Once rock 'n' roll took over and distortion became a defining sound of amplified bass and guitar (as well as the invention of the Precision Bass coming into its own), Ampeg's founder Everett Hull became more reclusive, not personally relating to this new musical movement, and assigned Jess Oliver to deal with this new generation of artists. Everett hated distortion, which is an amusing irony considering Ampeg's now-so-lidified foothold in the rock and metal worlds in addition to every other genre under the sun.

With the onslaught of so many boutique amp builders, the marketplace has become very crowded access to current information, past history, modern/vintage tech, and communications tools. This has resulted in not just a crowded marketplace for musical equipment but also a crowded marketplace for everything. Buying is voting in today's market. Vote for what you wish to continue to see manufactured or grown!

The best mini-stack for recording! Ampeg Micro-CL Stack

Retro city with that round and warm tone from days past! Ampeg Heritage R-12R Reverberocket

in recent years, but Ampeg still remains stronger than ever among musicians. Zane explains,

The art of designing fine musical amplifiers is as much a passion and intriguing subject of study as music is itself. Today's marketplace is a reflection of not only this, but also general population increase, globalization of information, and the globalization of technology. Not only are there more people in the world today than in 1949, but also more people have greater

I wanted to see how Ampeg deals with the emerging digital technology and what stake it has in today's market share. Zane assured me,

Analog amplification will never go away. There will never be anything else that can create the tone of tubes, other than tubes for instance. At the same time, digital technology is absolutely wonderful and wondrous and continues to evolve in unexpectedly amazing ways. With the advent of high-end modeling algorithms, direct digital recording, and continuously improving DSP quality from multiple manufacturers, one wonders where it will all go next. Combinations of digital amplifiers meshed with tube pre-amps are a great example of hybrid tech, which also continues to evolve and impress. Ampeg will always be open to innovation and taking the next steps forward to evolve. Our foundation is strong, but only because one man had the vision to innovate during a time when bass amplification did not exist. Today we have many visionaries that will continue to take Ampeg into the future utilizing current technology, creating new tech, and most importantly continuing to listen to our customers and create superior-sounding products that carry the 'round sound' Ampeg is known for.

Before we ended our conversation, Zane divulged on their upcoming products, "The new reissue of the V-4B is an amazing amplifier. Incredibly versatile, true analog Ampeg tone, 100 watts of power, half the weight of an SVT head, and doubles as one of the most kick-ass guitar amps you've ever played in addition to bass-guitar playing. From Austrian Crystal cleans to Louisiana Gumbo fuzz, and dialects in between, this thing will punch a hole in your

It's 1969 all over again, and the Stones are tearing it up!
Ampeg Heritage SVT-810E & SVT-CL

The Portaflex has made a come back and a face-lift!
Ampeg PF-500 Cab

The Ampeg System Selector for amplifiers and cabinets is one of the most useful tools to have in the studio to record various amp heads with cabinets!

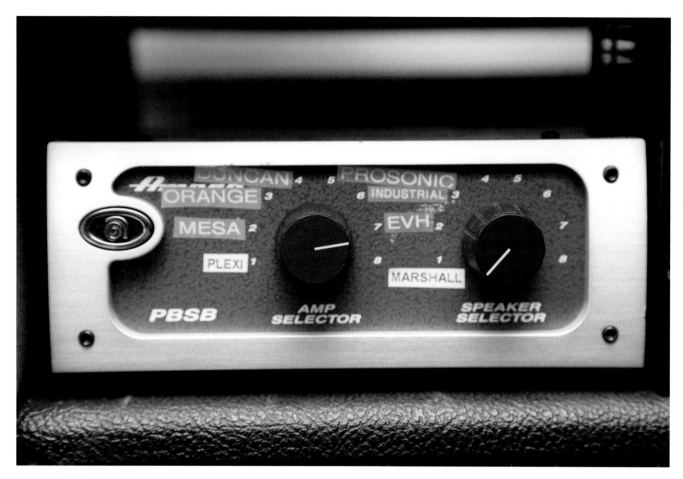

Ampeg PBSB Amp/Cabinet Selector: choose different heads to play through various speaker cabs.

expectations from a new/reissued tube amp . . . and your face. In a good way."

Carr

Carr amps may not be a household name, but nevertheless, founder Steve Carr has large aspirations for his company. Steve explains his humble beginnings.

I have been a musician since the beginning of high school (1977), and I started playing in bands that summer and I have not stopped! I got more into gear in the early nineties when I befriended a tech that helped me with my seventies non-master volume Marshall. We did some mods and general repair. He started me down the road of tube

Steve Carr, amp builder and entrepreneur, hard at work making his new creation

tinkering. I got a 1964 Blackface Deluxe Reverb shortly after that—and I was totally hooked. I read old electronics textbooks and whatever I could find on the early Internet! Then in 1997 I opened a repair and mod shop of my own and learned by doing (thanks to the plentiful guitar players of Chapel Hill, North Carolina, I always had work). Later, I designed an amp for myself. It combined the best of my Marshall and Fender in one box. This was the beginning of our Slant 6V model. Once I felt it was really good, I took it to a local music store, and they liked it so much they ordered two of them—I was blown away, and that is where I mark the beginning of Carr Amplifiers (fall 1998). As far as education, I went to Purdue for Aerospace Engineering and later UNC for Physics, but my experience as a musician is the thing I use most in amp design.

I was curious what prompted Steve to start an old-school amp company and how he planned on setting himself apart from other tube-amp manufacturers. He goes on to explain,

Inside Frankenstein's brain! The Viceroy

At the time I started Carr Amps, I was thinking one amp at a time. It was (and is) such a fun and exciting thing. As the orders slowly grew, I started to think of this more as a real business and began to take road trips, showing potential new dealers the amps. I believe I have something to contribute to the world of guitar tone—new twists and new emotive vibes. I draw from the best parts of classic designs and bring new utility while taking a step forward in both sonics and reliability. This too is how we are different than many of our competitors. Organic musicality and interactive feel are central here.

When asked if there was a classic amp design he aspired to he replied,

Yes, I often consider a classic amp I like and examine why it is such a fine instrument (generally amps pre-1980). Then I may bring in other parts of different classic amps, plus work on new features. Simplicity is very important to me and to our customers—intuitive controls with maximum useful range. I have a ton of experience with old Fenders and Marshalls. Recently I bought a 1964 Vox AC10 to gain a better understanding of the old Vox amps that used the EF86 pre-amp tube. Even if my final design is far from the original inspiration, having the classic amp as a springboard has been the surest approach for me.

As for the digital vs. analog issue, Steve went on to say, "For guitar amps I am all analog. To me, it feels the best under your fingers and is the most natural sounding. Also as a builder it is the most fun and satisfying architecture. Soldering point to point—touching each component as you build; this creates a living amp. Digital guitar amps are very convenient and can incorporate a ton of effects, but they are just that, a convenience, to me the musicality is very two dimensional, with little interactive feel. I prefer analog!"

As for new and exciting innovations from Carr,

I always have a number of ideas going, but I have to build them. Sometimes I think of a circuit, which seems like it will be great, but

Fine craftsmanship and attention to detail puts these amps a step ahead.

Steve Carr's Rambler amp—very rich

part further. It is very much a build-and-play method. Carr Amps has a fine group of guys working here. We build our own cabinets and handle everything from start to finish. My hope is this company continues to gain respect and market share while providing a good living for the craftsmen here and their families. As long as there are guitarists who value honest, evocative tone, Carr Amps will be there to serve them.

Carvin

During the nineties when I was endorsed by Carvin, I used to frequent its Hollywood store on Sunset Boulevard right next to the MESA/Boogie and across from Guitar Center. The San Diego headquarters was very gracious and made a number of amps for me back when I was touring. Many people don't realize that Carvin has been around for as long as Fender. Lowell Kiesel founded the Los Angeles company back in 1946 under the name, L. C. Kiesel Company. Kiesel later change the company name to Carvin, after his two eldest sons, Carson and Gavin. The company began by making pickups, guitars, and basses made by Lowell Kiesel, as well as rebadged guitars made by Harmony and Kay.

find it is not so good once I build it; then it is back to the drawing board. Or it may have an element that seems promising; I have to try and pull the good thing out and take that

The Classic Steve Vai Legacy 3 is screaming to be played!

Then in 1954 Carvin launched its first mail-order catalog, which is a business model that is still used today. During the sixties Carvin built most of its guitars from Hofner components. However, in 1970, Mark Kiesel took over Guitar Development and created the Custom Shop, designing guitars and basses again for the company. In 2015, Mark's son spearheaded a new line of guitars with the original logo name of Kiesel, honoring his grandfather Lowell.

Carvin has manufactured various guitar amplifiers through the years, from the classic tube-driven stacks that Steve Vai used with Frank Zappa to solid-state combos. I remember asking the company to place two Electro Voice 300-watt speakers in their 2x12" tweed combo, and they thought I was

The Carvin Legacy Mark I cranks hard overdrive, as well as clean tones.

nuts because of the weight. But the sound was so nice when overdriven, with a wonderful crystal-clean tone.

CeriaTone

CeriaTone spreads itself across the DIY, amp

CeriaTone's King Kong has two channels of thrust and tone!

shop, and boutique amp markets. It offers classic circuits, PTP boards, chassis, kits, and full working chassis. This is the brainchild of Nik S. Azam, who is an electrical engineer as well as an amplifier enthusiast. He explains:

> I went to college, with a degree in Electrical/ Computer Engineering, with an additional major in Psychology. As with most kids, music was a big part of my life, and of course, I tried to play the guitar (still trying!). At the time, i.e., early nineties, there were still lots of vintage amps being used in jamming studios back here, where kids go and jam with friends. It was only in college, in the USA, that I realized there was differentiation in value and quality, between vintage and new, as well as between tube and solid-state amps. So I read up a lot on

it, as well as dabbled in the circuits for a bit. There were still lots of amps to be had for cheap in the mid-nineties in the USA.

> I graduated, came back to Malaysia in late 1999, and started to look for the sought-after vintage amps, like Marshall Plexis, old Fenders, Voxes, etc., as well as vintage gear and effects. At this time, eBay was relatively new in the USA and definitely unknown in Malaysia. I did make quite a bit of money selling this vintage stuff on eBay, and I shipped them worldwide, as this old stuff could be found for dirt cheap. I did lots of repairs to old amps, mainly so I could sell them.

The CeriaTone King Kong's hot tubes and fat transformers make this beast rock!

In early 2000s, I stumbled on some forums where like-minded individuals meet to discuss amps. They also made their own amps, DIY style. I soon realized that there is a market to supply parts to these builders. Pretty soon, I began selling Turret boards and chassis online. As we progressed, I added things bit by bit, from boards, to passive parts, to transformers. And in 2003, we began selling complete amps, other than kits.

So Nik was prompted to start CeriaTone as he states,

I realized from dealing with vintage amps that the prices were quite high, and most musicians wouldn't be able to afford them. The DIY experience definitely taught me that they could be made, in the same style/quality as the old ones, but at lower costs. CeriaTone strives to provide the best value to musicians. We're not China, but we bring the good stuff.

When designing CeriaTone, Nik was inclined to use classic tones from older classic amp designs,

Definitely, you need to have a base to work with. A lot of times, musical trends tend to root from earlier times and influences. From there, we can tweak what we want it to be. Having said that, we cover lots of bases with our offerings. Due to our physical location, it is perhaps not possible for us to start a trend-setting signature sound. In order to survive as a business, we just make lots of amps, targeting a wide range of tastes.

When asked his opinion on analog versus digital technologies for amps Nik replied,

I keep an open mind. However, I still do not think digital technologies have achieved exact sameness of tube amps. When playing, it's not just about what you hear. It's how the amp reacts to the guitar in your hands, i.e. the feel, also matters. To those who say it's the same—get a tube amp of a specific model and then get the digital model that's supposed to mimic the former. Play it for a few days, weeks. Play it loud. Play it live. After that, only then come out to say whether they're the same or not. Don't come to your conclusions after playing it for five minutes, at grandma's volumes, in the bedroom, and without familiarization of the original.

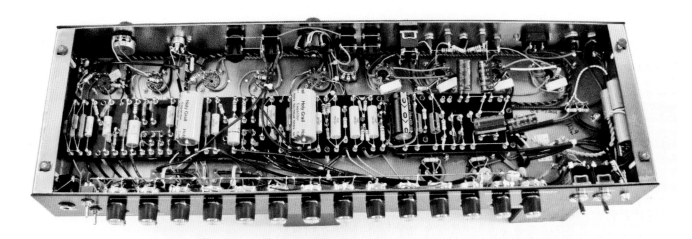

CeriaTone King Kong, inside the beast and the very workings of its mind

Nik is working on special innovative amps as he explains,

Currently, we're bringing lots of models to be in the lunchbox format, i.e., smaller, more portable, lower-power versions. For example, we have the OTS20 and the Son of Yeti.

The OTS20 runs 6V6s and has pretty much all the features of its bigger brothers, but made smaller and more affordable. To make this possible, we do not allow customization requests to the model. Circuit wise, it's really a design on its own and with its own tonal signature, distinct enough from the bigger models to be on its own and also not to cannibalize the sales of the higher priced models.

Our new offerings are also becoming more and more complex. Some have independent dual channels, with lots of modern features. Kind of hard to do with hand wiring on turret boards, but I guess that's what we do and are known for. In the near future, I'd really like to offer something very basic, features wise, but 100 watts or more. It will be pure, and it will be the antithesis to all these bedroom-playing-while-tap-dancing-on-100-pedals thing we currently have.

I hope to continue to do what we do now. I hope to be able to maintain, if not up the quality of our offerings. Beyond that, like corporate things, I don't pay much mind to. Of course, it's a business, but lots of problems we have currently are exactly because we try to complicate things. I make tube guitar amps. That's it.

Sometimes, you go to a store and wish there were more quality to the offerings.

The quality you want/expect is there, but priced at only an oil sheikh can pay.

We maintain that we continue to address the issue above: affordable quality.

Danelectro/Silvertone

In the fifties and sixties Danelectro's founder Nathan Daniels manufactured amplifiers in New Jersey. Nathan also manufactured OEM products for Montgomery Ward and Sears, like their Silvertone amps. Today we've seen a resurgence of the Silvertone amps for collectors. Many a guitarist from the Baby Boomers and

Danelectro 1953 Pioneer: it doesn't get more vintage than this for amps!

Danelectro 1953 Pioneer controls make you want to crank every knob up to eleven!

Danelectro 1953 Pioneer, backside of amp, featuring the tubes and controls

Sears 1958 Silvertone Model 1392—cool man's vintage!

The Sears 1958 Silvertone Model 1392 features both instrument and microphone input controls.

Generation X cut their teeth on these types of amps, like yours truly.

Divided By 13

The Divided By 13 Model CCC 9-15 112 has big tone in a small package for modern-day players.

Divided By 13 colorful tolex-covered amps ready to be shipped to lucky buyers

Fred Taccone grew up in Fullerton, California, the son of an aerospace engineer, whom he credits as a big influence in his life. Like many of his generation whose fathers were in World War II, he went to college for various degrees of engineering. Southern California was a haven for post-war veterans and their families, becoming the breeding ground for great minds both analytical and creative, to feed the great state with progressive ideas. It was also a great time for the aerospace programs and what inevitably would become the great space race to the moon during the next decades. So the stage was set for Fred to start tinkering with electronics at the early age of seven. By the time he was a teenager he started playing guitar and delving deeper in the electronic side of music with engineering. Right out of high school, Fred got a job with Fender and eventually worked for Music Man to further hone his skills, while at the same time attending college for electrical engineering.

Fast-forward to the mid-nineties; Taccone got a job repairing amps for Chris Ramano's Black Market

on the West Coast and met a lot of influential guitarists along the way. His involvement with guitarist Rusty Anderson inspired his FTR 37. In 2001, as luck would have it, Rusty was playing the 2001 *Concert for New York City* to benefit the 9/11 victims, in Paul McCarthy's band, and he brought along the Divided By 13 amps onstage. With such worldwide exposure, the amps started to take off, and Fred was rushed with new orders for amps. During this time there were not as many boutique amp designers, so it was a wide-open field still for tube amps. Fred states, "Ya know, it's like a lot of things, we all know it's a pizza; one guy gets the blue ribbon, and the other one doesn't. So I'm not reinventing the wheel here, I've got my own take on things. I've got some amps that are influenced by amps from the past, like Marshalls and Fenders, and some that break new ground."

Fred also points out that what most people hear are modified Fenders or Marshalls; even though it may carry the brand name, it's usually not stock from the factory. "I've been doing this a very long time and been fortunate. When you're a kid and you go to your junior high dance back in 1967, and the guy is playing a gold-top Les Paul and a small-box fifty-watt Marshall half stack, Cry Baby and Fuzz Face, I mean you pretty much

Divided By 13 Pippen 112. It sounds as beautiful as it looks.

Divided By 13's Fred Taccone at Abbey Road, having fun

Brian Ray from Paul McCartney's band with his Divided By 13 amp—is he flipping us off?

This Egnater Armageddon Head is ready to shred and take no prisoners!

got it right there. Plus I'm a music fan, and I have been hardcore about it since I could remember." As he pointed out, this was all just an accident; it took a lot of years to achieve his success.

Egnater

Bruce Egnater's journey started over four decades ago as a Jimi Hendrix and Cream-loving guitarist. In his words,

My interest in music, particularly guitar, probably started when I was around eleven years old. I was the kid who had to take everything apart. But the real story started when I was twelve or thirteen years old. I used to ride my bike to the local Topp's Department Store and buy every new record that had guitar, bass, and drums. I still have most of the vinyl records. I vividly

remember finding two new records around 1969 that really stood out. One was The Jimi Hendrix Experience (*Are You Experienced*), and the other was Cream (*Fresh Cream*). Those two albums truly changed my life. I know, today those are just old classics. Back then, they were the most innovative and radical guitar records I had ever heard. I knew right then I wanted to be a rock star. Needless to say, things did not work out exactly as I had hoped. Along the way, I really got interested in the gear. Of course, I couldn't leave things alone and started really seriously studying how and why amps and audio stuff worked. This was way before computers and the Internet, so I would write letters to every amp company requesting schematics. Many sent them. Some didn't. Needless to say, I couldn't help myself, so I started tinkering with my own amps. I really learned a lot just tinkering. Back then you were basically on your own, because everyone was trying to figure it out at the same time. The industry was quite new, and everything was in its infancy. There were no standards for anything. There was no such thing as a vintage "Plexi" Marshall. They were all Plexi Marshalls because they were new, and they blew up every day!

After attending the University of Detroit Engineering School in the mid-1970s, Bruce opened his first repair shop. He specialized in repairing and modifying amps as well as keyboards and guitars. It was here that he really began to expand both his knowledge and skills as an amp guy. Boogie had just come out with its innovative Mark II models that had clean and overdrive modes, but shared the tone controls. Bruce remembers,

I thought this was too limiting. I wanted a tube amp with two totally separate channels, but nobody made one, so I made my own. I thought, "What the heck, I can do that." To my surprise it worked and sounded pretty good. I used it for many years in my progressive rock playing days. Other players heard my tone, and I ended up making amps for them. I guess you could say that was the beginning of my amp-building obsession. The obsession with amps began to really consume me and started to turn into what would become a full-time career. I continued, relentlessly of course, to find new sounds and features in amps I would build. This led to the development of the four-channel IE4 pre-amp and the TOL model amps, which were all hand-built in our tiny shop in Detroit. The demand for hotrod and for me to modify other players' amps became pretty huge. Eventually, I found myself modifying my own amps to create new and different tones. My goal became to design a tube amp that would work for every player

The Egnater Vegeance Head makes any metal head proud!

in every situation. The ingenious result, if I do say so myself, was the modular amp. With this design, the power-amp section stays constant while the pre-amps are modular, meaning they can be changed in and out of the amp with ease. This gave musicians the flexibility they sought to have totally different-sounding channels in one amp.

So obviously Bruce was all set to start Egnater and set the amp world on fire, as he states, "Starting Egnater was simply the logical progression from my amp obsession to wanting to make amps for others."

The Egnater REBEL 30 112 MARK II takes you on a tonal journey from blues to hard rock!

After getting encouragement from local musicians, it appeared I had no choice but to go into business. I guess the desire to push the boundaries of fifty-year-old tube technology would set us apart from some others. I try to be an innovator, not a copier."

When asked if any classic amps played an important role in his own designs, he proclaimed,

Egnater Tweaker 40, for those of you who love switches and extra controls to dial your sound

Of course, any designer draws from the past. The classic Fender/Marshall/Vox circuits certainly have influenced all modern-day tube-amp builders. It is simply unavoidable. Whenever it is time to design a new product, the first question I ask myself is, *what will be the thing that will make it uniquely Egnater?* A sound or feature that will set it apart. The Egnater TOL amps and IE4 pre-amp were some of the first tube amps that used MIDI for channel switching. Each model since then has some unique, useful feature that makes it different or special. I came up with the tube-mix feature that allows you to blend two different pairs of power tubes; switchable four-level power settings per channel was another. The Tweaker models opened a whole new world of sounds with an almost endless number of tonal combinations. The Rebel sort of set a new standard for "lunchbox" amps. Even our newest pedals offer features and sounds not typically found in guitar pedals. Our modular amps are quite unique to the amp world.

And what does Egnator think of the new digital technology for amp designs,

Long ago guitar players were all afraid that disco would replace them. Clearly that did not happen. I think there is a place in the world for everyone, including different technologies. The digital-audio world is clearly the future, but I also believe analog, in particular tube technology will have its place in the music world for quite a long time. I am inspired by the number of young players who are interested in tube amps. We even have many young players attending our amp-building classes. There just isn't anything quite like a great, old cranked-up tube amp.

ENGL

ENGL is a high-gain German amp manufacturer whose fans are mostly in the heavy-metal genre. Ritchie Blackmore was one of the first high-profile guitar players whom ENGL endorsed. It

Steve Morse and Vivian Campbell with their signature ENGL Amp heads

Steve Morse and Dave LaRue tearing it up live with a little help from ENGL

Ron Bumblefoot Thal and friend evoke shred confidence; you go, Ron!

ENGL Straight combo from my buddy Geoff Gray at Far & Away Studios: I've played through this beast, gain for days!

Epiphone Valve Junior with the Bit Mo Modification

Epiphone Valve Junior, modified to have more gain and clarity with a push-pull knob and added mini-toggle switch

seems that ENGL is cutting into Marshall's market share when it comes to heavy-metal tone with endorsements from: Glen Tipton from Judas Priest, Bumblefoot from Guns N' Roses, Chris Broderick from Megadeth, and the list goes on. My good friend Steve Morse is also a devoted endorser with his own signature amp model, tone for days!

Epiphone

Like Epiphone's guitars, its amps have had a place in American music for decades. Many guitarists during the 1940s big band era used the Electar Zephyr. But when the guitar came into its own in the sixties, Epiphone amps such as the Galaxie and Comet became instant successes. One of the most impressive innovations in the sixties was the Epiphone Professional amp. It actually integrated all of the amp controls onto the accompanying Epiphone guitar pick guard. Fast-forward to the 2000s with the release of the

Epiphone Valve Junior head and combo, which has an impressive sound for only a five-watt amp. A third-party company called BitMo even makes modification kits to dial in the tone for your Valve Junior.

Fargen

Hard to believe that Fargen amps have now been around for fifteen years now. Time really flies when you're a musician. When they first came on

Fargen High Gain Series head, reminiscent to the Marshall JMP days

Fargen High Gain, back of head, sporting modern features such as FX Loop and FX on/off toggle switch

the market, I remember reading about the amps and their recreation of the classic British tones from Marshall's Plexi amps. Ben Fargen's interest in electronics dates back to his high school days in ROP electronics class.

We actually had an amazing electronics teacher who was a musician, and he really pushed me to learn more. We built some simple graded MI projects like a fuzz pedal and he would have us bring in broken pieces like an old, small clone a friend had that wasn't working. It was invaluable in regard to learning the basics of electronics and soldering . . . it definitely sparked my curiosity about the industry. As far as actual tube amps are concerned . . . I had a small stable of vintage tube amps that I owned in my twenties, and they all started having issues. At that time in Sacramento, California, there wasn't anyone I really trusted with my tubes amps . . . so I dug in myself with help from a few books/ Internet and learned the basics of tube audio . . . at least enough to do some simple repairs. At that point I got the bug to build a couple DIY clones that I dragged around town to gigs . . . this led to other local players hiring me to repair their vintage amps as well as a few simple custom amp builds.

Ben remembers when he first started the company and why,

At the time I officially started Fargen, the Internet was still in its infancy (1994–1995). You had to dig a lot deeper to get info about how tube amps operate and how to build them at that time . . . books and such. I really enjoyed the vintage repair aspect, and that background helped me get a quick handle on how the classics were constructed as well as some of their

shortcomings. I was working a job that was four- to ten-hour days, so I had quite a bit of free time on my days off. I took that opportunity to start Fargen amps as a fun hobby that started to make some extra money. In three short years, I had so much business that it was a crossroads . . . either quit my day job or stop building amps, so I took a chance, and here we are seventeen years later. I think the key point that separates us from other companies is my ear for great tone and my constant search for better-sounding parts and materials. After all these years I am still willing to try out new parts, transformers, speakers, etc., and if a new part beats out what we are currently using in tone and quality, I'll move to that part; cost is no object. If you lose the passion and the desire to continually make the amps sound and operate better . . . it's time to stop and move on to something else.

Fargen Town House twenty-watt combo, featuring a 1x12" and retro tolex

When designing Fargen amps, Ben was drawn to certain classic tones as templates.

The Fargen Jazz Custom SE features a specially designed circuit for jazz shredders.

As any amp builder has to, you must follow the classic designs to a certain extent, because players are classically conditioned to like a certain sound based on famous players and recordings using those amps. For some reason, I was challenged early in my career by many customers who requested me to build very specific custom variations that other amp builders at the time were not willing to entertain, so in some ways I was flying without a net when someone asked for a hybrid design that had never been built before. I quickly became known as the go-to guy in the industry for anyone wanting a custom-shop variation that no one else was willing to build; even my competitors were sending guys to me for custom builds. I think that helped me establish a name in the industry much quicker than otherwise just building straight Fender, Marshall, and Vox clones.

As for that million-dollar question on how digital technology stacks up against traditional analog when designing amps, Ben responded,

If it's a quality instrument, I view it as just another tool in the toolbox, especially when it

Fargen High Gain Series head, lovely stacked heads to capture the perfect tone

comes to recording. I have a very in-depth studio and recording background, so I never have hated or bagged on guitar-modeling technology the way maybe a straight "guitar player" who doesn't have a need for the resource or solution would. I do some cue and sound library recordings on a fairly regular basis, so in the middle of the night, when you need to lay down a quick "idea" track, a POD or other modeler comes in real handy. Is it the end-all tone? Of course not, but it's great as a sketch pad or a way to capture the vibe or idea, then I go back and track the part with a tube amp as soon as time and volume allows for the final track, etc.

Fargen has some new designs in the works, for all you anxious guitarists.

I am currently getting ready to release the Fargen Mini Plex MKIII. This is the newest version of

our professional low-volume Apt/Studio Brit amp. I am also putting the finishing touches on two new Fargen dual-channel series. These new versions are the next generation of our Dual Classic and Dual British Classic series amps. Both of these amps fuse an ultimate blackface tone with a fully foot-switchable classic and high-gain British sounds; extras like full-tube buffered FX loop and smaller, compact overall footprint will be standard.

Harmony

Harmony was mostly known as a major player in the affordable guitar-manufacturing world. Its amps were less popular and even considered lower on the totem pole as far as quality. However, with that being said, many a student from the Baby Boomers and Gen Xers cut their teeth on these amps, until they could afford to spend the cash on a Marshall.

Ibanez

Much like Harmony, Ibanez is well known for its guitars and less so for its amps. However, it has a new Tube Screamer amp with an interesting twist.

Classic Harmony amp model H306 from 1962

1962 Harmony amp model H306 backside, showing controls and those glowing GE tubes

Ibanez TSA5TVR Class A 5-Watt Combo

These amps come with the legendary Tube Screamer circuit built in. For instance, the TSA5TVR is an all-tube, Class-A, five-watt combo with an actual TS808 Tube Screamer built into the front end of the amp. The TS808 circuit is combined with a 12AX7 pre-amp tube and the 6V6GT power tube. The combo is loaded with an eight-inch Jensen C8R speaker, along with built-in Accutronics Reverb for spring reverb.

Ibanez TSA15 combo with a genuine Tube Screamer circuit built into the amp

Industrial

Industrial Custom 15, beautifully made and hand wired with tons of punch and overdrive

Below is my interview/review of Industrial Amps that originally appeared in Premier Guitar in 2008.

Industrial Amps Rock 120

Today it seems as though there's a boutique amp manufacturer around every corner. Don't get me wrong—boutique amps aren't a bad thing, but a great many of them focus on recreating the same types of tones that we've heard before, sapping all of the meaning from the word, "boutique." If you were to be objective about it, you could make the argument that Leo Fender's Bassman was the forefather of modern guitar amplification—it was the very amp that Jim Marshall and Randall Smith [MESA/Boogie] hot-rodded to make their own famous amps. But with so many small builders basing their sounds off these designs, where is the room for improvement?

With that said, I literally bumped into a mom and pop operation by the name of Industrial Amps at the Boston Guitar Festival, hosted by none other than Premier Guitar. I was wearing a Marshall T-shirt when I ran into JoAnn Niekrewicz, the co-owner of Industrial Amps; seeing my shirt's logo, she shouted through the crowd, "Try our amps—they are Marshall killers!"

Needless to say, it was a bold statement, but curiosity got the best of me; I immediately sat down and tried all of Industrial Amps. Plugging into models like the Rock 120, Blues 60, Crunch 15, and Overdrive 15, I soon noticed that each amp had its own special sound. The Blues 60 had a nice, hollow blues tone, while the Crunch 15 and the Overdrive 15 seemed perfect for studio recording, providing dynamic tone saturation. When I arrived at the Rock 120, I was thoroughly blown away by the depth of crunch that it produced, especially when it was played through the IA extended 4x12" speaker cabinet, loaded with Celestion Vintage 30s. To explore this amp further, I had them send the Rock 120 combo to my studio, so I could really put it through its paces in a working environment.

Industrial Rock

Right out of the box, the Rock 120 is a striking piece of modern, industrial design. The amp is constructed in a white tolex case made from 3/4" true eleven-ply hardwood birch, with the speakers enclosed behind a heavy-duty grill made from 1/4" aluminum for kick-proof protection. As for the cabinet itself, Industrial Amps Designer Tony Niekrewicz works closely with a non-profit organization called Living Classrooms in Baltimore, Maryland. The program gives out-of-school youth, from ages sixteen to nineteen, a chance to learn carpentry hands on in a practical work environment.

The tubes, transformers, and capacitors all cleverly reside behind a 1/4" thick glass, so you can experience the mesmerizing glow of electronics at work. As an added bonus, the Rock 120 is tour ready, boasting a set of large, riveted, zinc-coated handles with grips on both sides of the case, as well as four caster wheels for easy transport. Electronically, the amp features 120 watts, two channels—Classic and Heavy—point-to-point hand wiring and an open-back cabinet fitted with two 12-inch Celestion 80s. The amp itself is powered by four premium 12AX7s, four EL34s, one 12AT7 for reverb, and a solid-state rectifier tube.

Turning my attention first to the Classic channel, I ran several guitars through it. In particular, my Gibson double-neck Jimmy Page Model produced a gorgeous, ringing tone, much like the tone you hear on the Birds song, "8 Miles High" or even the Zeppelin classic, "The Song Remains the Same." A word of advice: when using double humbuckers, you'll have to back off on the guitar's volume a bit, so you won't overdrive the amp. What worked best for me was a Fender Strat. Through the Classic channel,

the single coils produced a very smooth and fresh reverberation, similar to that of a Fender Deluxe.

Switching over to the Heavy channel produced a genuinely heavy bass response, perfect for shaking your tree. Overdriven, the Rock 120 is a cross between a classic MESA/Boogie Mark II and a Soldano amp. I used the amp on several recording sessions and even had Leslie West [of Mountain] play through the amp. He was very impressed with the amp's gain—this coming from a guy who can never have too much gain. The notes were expressive and had an authentic, singing overtone; for those of you who remember the short-lived Fender Prosonic amp, this amp has a similar, driving tone.

The Rock 120 also recorded very well, especially using a Les Paul Goldtop with a Seymour Duncan 1959 humbucker in the bridge position and a Duncan Custom in the neck position. The tones were very saturated, but without the muddiness that some overdriven amps generate, due to the Mercury Magnetics transformer inside—designed to provide both clarity and bottom growl. It has that MESA/Boogie singing tone and is great with pinch harmonics. The Treble, Bass, and Presence controls are quite responsive, and unlike some amps, each one of the knobs really affects the tone. As an added bonus, the Heavy channel features a Gain control and a Master, so you don't have to sacrifice your eardrums for sweet tone.

There is lots to love here, and IA has added plenty of little touches that will make the purchasing decision easy. Each amp features dual-speaker outs, voltage and ohm selectors, military spec components, and even, "severe duty Honeywell explosion-proof aircraft-quality switches." How much more rock n' roll can you get?

The Final Mojo

Being an avid collector of vintage tube amps, I'm always skeptical of new products claiming to have

The Industrial Custom 15 uses Mercury transformers for that huge tone!

superior sound. But my experience with Industrial Amps opened my ears to what small-amp builders can achieve. While the price may be equivalent to other boutique amp models out there, the Rock 120 definitely gives you a lot more, in terms of sound and power. You won't find this amp in Guitar Center, Sam Ash, or any of the other commercial retailers—this a true underground find.

Jet City

The Jet City twenty-watt head has all of the tone and crunch you'd expect!

Jet City Amplification was launched in 2009 by amp connoisseur Mike Soldano and Douglas White. The whole idea of the amp line was to give guitarists affordable and great-sounding amps. Jet City Amplification also manufactures pedals, attenuators, and an isolation cabinet. It even has a company called AmpFactory for custom hot-rodding amps. It boasts using big, heavy, custom-wound transformers and thick PCBs with wide, two-ounce copper traces for reliability and tone. That's old school. That's my school!

The Jet City 100HDM has two channels of Soldano tone and 100 watts of pure tube power!

Douglas White explains:

Working with such brands as Gibson, Epiphone, Crate, Ampeg, and Blackheart, I learned quite a bit about manufacturing and marketing guitar amplifiers across a period of several years. I met Michael many years ago, when I put together a small team for Gibson, and we were looking for someone to do some assembly here in Seattle. During that project, we became good friends, and when I was ready to start up Jet City, it was very easy for us to decide to do it together. We started with the basic Soldano formula—designs of Mike's, which were already complete and in production under his brand. Shortly after launch, I expanded the range into some other areas, but starting with Soldano's designs was what put us into the market. His name opened a lot of doors for us, and his designs are very buildable and robust. It was that strong platform that gave us the starting point.

that's allowing some great tones to be produced live and in studio. What sets JCA apart from some of the others is our simplicity and robustness of design—we are all about pure, simple tone and function." And when it comes to new technologies Doug explains, "Both are great—I don't see it as versus, but as a nice array of available technologies.

The Jet City AMP SWITCH is fantastic to have for recording or live to feed two different amps for stereo.

Jet City 2112RC MKII 20 watts—all tube single-channel tube-driven reverb

Doug has an optimistic outlook on today's marketplace, "It is very exciting! Today's guitarist has many great tools within affordable reach, and

Jet City 48CV: stack 'em to the heavens to be heard around the world!

Jet City twenty-watt head with digital presets and knob controls

Jet City 5212RC—fifty watts, all tube with two channels, including tube-driven effects loop and reverb

Jet City Jettenuator, a hand-wired 100-watt attenuator

Most of what we do is old-school, analog technology, but we play around with some digital stuff—both are wonderful."

When asked the ingredients for great guitar overdrive tone Doug replied, "The guitar and the amp and, of course, a quality speaker. The player needs some skill too. So I guess I only left out the pedal. I don't think pedals are necessary to great tone, but they sure are nice to have and can add a lot to the player's flexibility."

Jim Kelly

Jim Kelly Line Amp overdrive, tone, and presence are all you need!

The short-lived Jim Kelley Amplifiers of the 1980s created a cult following because of their heavy-duty construction and quality build. According to noted amp collector Aspen Pitt, Kelly was the first company to use Groove Tubes in production. It even sported built-in attenuators to use the output tubes to create overdrive. Unfortunately Jim never took it any further and quit the business,

The rare Jim Kelly reverb amp has grown a cult following through the years.

so these amps are hard to come by, except eBay from time to time.

Kustom

In the seventies, my definition of being a rock star, from a teenager's point of view, was owning one of those red-, white-, blue-, or black-padded Kustom tuck-n-roll amp stacks. They looked awesome, encased with glittering padded covers that screamed, "loud and proud!" So, I dragged my old Yamaha 2x12" combo and 2x15" large cabinet to an upholstery man and had him cover them with padded red vinyl material. Maybe it was the time or just my age, but man it was sooooo cool!

But back to the book, the Kustom story started with a man named Charles "Bud" Ross. In 1964 he made the first Kustom amp, featuring 2x15" speakers mounted next to each other, horizontally covered in white sparkle with a matching head. The amps were nicked named "Tuck-N-Roll" because of the unique padded material that was used to cover the amp. The covering was artificial leather that was used for upholstering seats in hot-rod cars at the time. This was immediately a big selling point to the public, even though the amps were

Kustom Model TR12L solid-state amp, tuck-n-roll groovy-and-sparkling design, featuring a harmonic clipping button

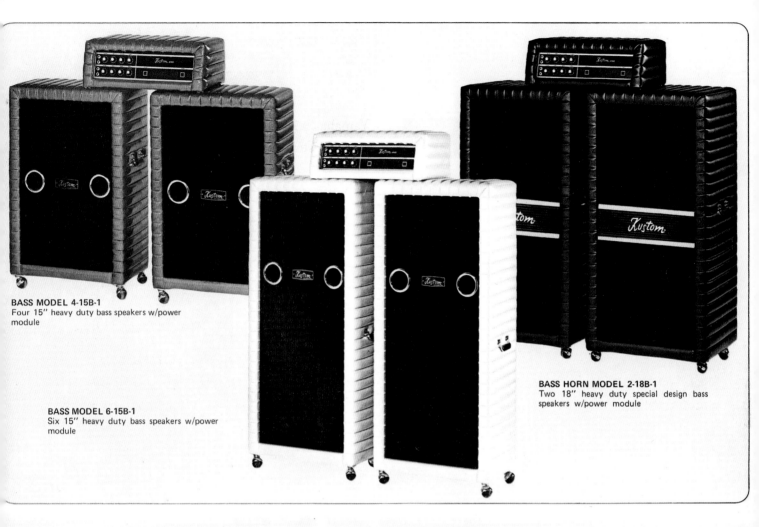

BASS 500

The 500 bass series are the sound giants. They're the biggest and best combination of power, performance and complete control yet. One speaker cabinet contains its own amplifier, and they combine to give you 500 watts. Any number of additional cabinets may be added to increase your sound requirements without affecting balance or quality of the total system.

BASS MODEL 4-15B-1
Four 15" heavy duty bass speakers w/power module

BASS MODEL 6-15B-1
Six 15" heavy duty bass speakers w/power module

BASS HORN MODEL 2-18B-1
Two 18" heavy duty special design bass speakers w/power module

Kustom Amp catalog from 1972: I loved these catalogs, just made me drool!

solid state as opposed to the traditional tube technology. Ross owned the company until 1972 and then sold it to Baldwin Pianos.

Lafayette

Lafayette Radio Electronics dates back to the 1920s as a consumer-radio manufacturer. It established itself as a major mail-order catalog business selling various electronic components directed to amateur radio enthusiasts and hobbyists. The products they offered were stereos, two-way radios, and CBs. It moved into the electronic musical instrument business, however, mostly made by other manufacturers with their names placed on the instruments from

Lafayette amp from the defunct Indigo Ranch recording studios

guitars to pedals to amplifiers. Its musical products were very basic and were targeted for beginners or students. But with that being said, its most famous product was the Uni-Vibe used by the late, great Jimi Hendrix and Stevie Ray Vaughan.

Amp sporting the Lafayette name, most likely made by Harmony or another manufacturer

Lectrolab

1956 Lectrolab 500 made by Sound Projects Company in Illinois

Lectrolab was a brand name for amplifiers made by a company in Illinois called Sound Projects. It

began manufacturing amps during the big band era and continued until the British Invasion. In those years it produced twenty-four amp models, from one-channel three-watt combos to two-channel, twenty-five-watt heads featuring reverb and tremolo. Like any good sixties amp manufacturer, it also manufactured a fuzz pedal and guitar pickups. Its amps and accessories were available through popular department stores of the day and by mail order for affordable prices.

1956 Lectrolab 500 with chicken-head knobs

Line 6

Line 6 introduced the guitar world to the first digital modeling amplifiers and took musicians by storm with POD multi-effects. It also carries Variax guitars, StageScape live sound workstations, StageSource loudspeakers, and AMPLIFi amps. I think most guitarists know Line 6 one way or another. It produces creative tools and, like one of our designers mentioned, can be used as sketchpads for musical ideas and sounds.

Line 6 amp head with tube designed by Bogner

Backside of Line 6 DT25 amp head, where the tube section was designed by Bogner amps

Magnatone

1965 Magnatone M7, a beautifully yellowed speaker weave from fifty years of tone!

If you want to know about Magnatone amps, just ask Neil Young; his devotion to the amp still lives strong today. It spans back to the thirties when Magna Electronics manufactured amps along with guitars. Delbert Dickerson started the company under the name the Dickerson Musical Instrument Company in Southern California. During the fifties and sixties, it armed its amps with vibrato, which was used by popular guitarists of the time like Buddy Holly. In 1946 Art Duhamell acquired the company and renamed the company Magnatone. Under Art's supervision, the company experienced its biggest growth and innovation until it closed its door in the seventies. In 2013, Ted Kornblum, formally of Ampeg and St. Louis Music, revived Magnatone.

Matchless Independence features thirty-five watts and three channels with backlit controls

Matchless

Way before the craze of boutique amp builders came into fruition, Matchless amps spearheaded the market in 1989 with versatile tone-driven amplifiers. Phil Jamison, Chief Operating Officer recalls the history:

Originally I started out as a guitarist, and a few years after finishing at GIT in 1988,

I worked at a company that did cartage and tech work. That's when I became really interested in sound and what the session guys were using. I figured the more I knew about amps and sound, it would really help round me off as a working guitarist. So, following the tech gig, I got a job at an amp company. Basically all I learned there was just the physical part of it, wiring, stuffing boards, very basic stuff. After that job ended I got a call from someone saying Matchless needed to hire someone, and I went in and met with Rick Perrotta, the cofounder. That was in late 1992. I fell in love with the amps, and I was eager to learn every aspect of building them.

Matchless Independence has hand-wired glowing glass tubes that no POD can match!

Unlike other manufacturers, Matchless did not have to change its business model with technology.

Technology hasn't really changed Matchless. I think Matchless really has its roots in simplicity. It seems some of the modern technology is trying to make a very simple thing very complex for the sake of avoiding tubes or offering too many bells and whistles. When I designed the Independence 35, I wanted to make something that could play a wide

range of music in one package and still keep it as pure and simplistic as possible. I heard too many amps with multiple channels that couldn't do them all well at the same time. I spent a couple of years perfecting this design and making it sound great as three individual amps. When I designed the DC30 Reverb, I had to come up with a way for both channels and the reverb not to interfere with one another, so I used switching relays similar to what I did in the Independence.

The Matchless Phoenix features two contrasting pre-amp channels for ultimate tone!

When asked if there were any classic tones used as templates when designing new amps, Phil replied,

Really what I've always done is go for sounds. I've never once taken an amp and looked at it and thought, "How can I duplicate this?" I hear about people buying amps just to copy them, and that sort of thing doesn't appeal to me. Matchless had made a name for itself in taking elements of early sixties Vox amps and melding them together and improving the construction and reliability. So in that regard, I see how it's a positive thing to take an old design and try to improve upon it. What I see a lot nowadays is people taking a current design and making it cheaper. I don't think that's really the same thing.

The Matchless DC30, the amp that started the whole company, is still the Flagship!

As far as the digital vs. analog question, Jamison responded, "Digital recording and plug-ins have certainly gotten much better over the years. But, I have not heard a digital amp or plug-in for a guitar sound that I was comfortable with. The cleans have gotten better, but there is still an element I hear

Matchless King Cobra, featuring both tremolo and reverb

that is missing. And I have yet to hear a gain sound or a touch response element in digital." And the future looks bright for new, innovative products, "I am currently working on several things at the moment, and in our tradition, I will keep it as pure as possible. I just finished up the design of the second generation of Avalon 30 Reverb amps, and they are without question some of the best-sounding amps we have ever made at Matchless. I couldn't be happier with the Avalon 30s."

MESA/Boogie

MESA/Boogie Mark II B, the sweetest tone and sustain in a combo

MESA/Boogie began in 1969 by repair tech Randall Smith in Petaluma, California. It all started with a Fender Princeton amp that he modified, taking a Fender Bassman amplifier section and installing it in the Princeton. At the same time he replaced the dinky, stock ten-inch speaker in the Princeton with a twelve-inch one. This inherently gave the amp more gain and volume. I guess it all starts with a Fender Bassman circuit, as Jim Marshall found out as well. Supposedly after playing the new Frankenstein amp, Carlos Santana said, "This thing boogies!" Hence the legacy was born! This was truly the birth of the boutique amp makers, which became an empire for Randall. From there he added an extra gain-input stage, now known as the cascade design. With this new design MESA/Boogie had the first high-gain amp, later known as the Mark I, released in 1972. The unique power-tube configuration, named Simul-Class, was introduced by Boogie in the eighties and was offered in the Mark II C and C+ series. In layman terms, it allows you to switch between two different types of power tubes, usually 6L6s and EL34s, each with its own inherent sound and tone. The 6L6s were commonly used in American amps like Fenders, and the EL84s were typically used in British amps like Marshalls. The ability to switch between the two was very revolutionary for the time.

The Mark I had many variations in the seventies, featuring slider EQ controls, reverb, ornate Koa wood jointed cabinets, and those handsome wicker grills. In 1978 Mark II was introduced, followed by the Mark III in the eighties, which offered

more gain and innovations, like the Studio .22 and Son of Boogie. MESA/Boogie started to cater to heavy-metal guitarists with its ultra high-gain amp heads. The later Mark series found its way to huge arenas, delivering loud and prominent tones with the likes of Metallica. In the 2000s MESA/Boogie took overdrive a step further with the release of the Rectifier and Mark V.

The MESA/Boogie Son of Boogie, a.k.a. SOB, is a great-sounding amp very reminiscent of a Plexi tone!

MESA/Boogie 50 Caliber. True to it's name, it hits you hard and heavy!

Orange

Orange CR120 solid-state head with PPC212 cabinet, simply fantastic sounding!

In 1968, Cliff Cooper opened the Orange Shop in East London, where he sold second-hand guitars and amplifiers, as well as a recording studio he had built in the basement. At the time, no distributors wanted to supply him with new gear or amplifiers, so he took it upon himself to design his own amps, and the Orange Amp was born. It also didn't hurt that he had a background in electronics. From there he hired Radio Craft, owned by Mat Mathias, to build the first amps and the rest is history. From the start, the Orange Amp stood out because of its well-built components, bright-orange color, picture graphics above the knobs, and psychedelic logo. The brand took off, and sales shored well into the seventies until the company went out of business in 1979. Fortunately, Orange came back with a vengeance in the early 2000s and is still going strong today. Its models like the AD15/30, Rockerverb, Tiny Terror, Dark

Terror, and even their solid-state amp CR120 kicks serious booty.

When I was in London, recording a solo record for Instinct Records in the nineties, I actually went down to Rhodes Music store on Denmark Street, bought an Orange AD15 combo, and had it shipped back to the states. It was a big deal at the time, because finding a brand-new Orange Amp in the United States was next to none. The whole experience was surreal. Supposedly they were making these amps in the basement, and I had to have one. When I got it home, I found that I needed a bit more gain for lead tones, so I took it to an amp modifier in San Fernando Valley. He added an extra 12AX7 to the gain stage, and man it rips; this was way before the Tiny Terror series was out, I might add.

The Orange OR15 and 2x12" cabinet cranks up the classic overdrive tones!

To get the inside lowdown, I spoke to Orange Tech Director Adrian Emsley. He was kind enough to explain his background,

My dad showed me how to use a soldering iron when I was a kid back in the seventies and talked me through the troubleshooting process. I studied many books on tube electronics and modified many British fifty-watt and 100-watt heads in the mid to late eighties. These mods included getting more gain, tweaking them to suit a certain player's preference, switching systems, etc. I then went on to restoring vintage Marshalls, Voxes, and tweed Fenders, using original parts, which led me to appreciate real tone over high-gain modifications. I started building a small number of vintage flavored thirty-, forty-five-, and fifty-watt heads in mahogany boxes for certain players in the early nineties. I started doing work for Orange in 1997 and set about bringing the brand back into favor.

Adrian explains his designing process and how he revisited classic tones,

The template for the first Orange amps I designed was based on the seventies' Orange tone at a more usable power. These amps were the AD15 and AD30 and were not high-gain amps. I wanted to recreate a classic Orange crunch tone and establish it with the guitar-playing public before taking the brand into high-gain territories. Those amps had a very strong type mid-range, combined with the superior saturation of EL84s.

Adrian goes on to explain how the amp market has become so crowded, "There are many boutique guitar amps made today that have absolutely no originality and are simply JTM45 or

Orange Tiny Terror hit the market with the perfect high-gain tone!

Orange Rockerverb 50 MKII, four stages of unadulterated filth

Orange Dark Terror takes you even further than the Tiny Terror, with loads of Orange grit.

tweed fender copies. More attention to detail is applied to the way they look inside than to how they actually sound, IMO. Having said that, there are a few interesting and decent-sounding amps like 65amp, Zinky (Supro), and Satellite, etc. All three of those guys really know what they're doing and make products with some originality for sure."

As for the analog versus digital preferences, he states, "I don't personally like to mix the two in one package, especially tube amps with digital circuitry. I like to keep the tube amps 100 percent tube and the solid-state amps 100 percent solid state. My two main reasons for this are: (1) trades description and (2) tubes run at much higher voltages than most solid-state devices." And as far as his favorite Orange amps, Adrian prefers the Tiny Terror or a Dual Terror, "I like the fact that all of the overdrive is made push pull, and I tend to use those amps

Orange AD-15: this is the baby I bought in London years ago and had an extra 12AX7 put in the gain stage.

with the volume on ten, tone on ten, gain at twelve o'clock, which means that the EL84s and speakers are handling most of the resulting overdrive."

Orange CR120 Head, don't let the solid-state fool you; this sounds better than some tube heads.

The Orange AD30 Twin Channel delivers that bluesy crunch tone.

Pignose

The Classic Pignose mini-amp ran on batteries and could be taken anywhere.

Here is the Pignose story told by its founder Richard Edlund.

Wayne Kimbell and I were partners doing graphics and photography for the rock and roll trade from about 1968 to 1969. I saw a five-watt amplifier at Pacific Radio, and the idea hit me right there. I made the first one in an English leather cedar men's cologne box. My friend Warren Zevon (I shot his first album cover) was recording his second album at Wally Heider's studio with Peaveys turned up to eleven to get feedback—he was making enemies in nearby sessions. I said, "Try the Pignose." He fell in love with it and finished all of his album sessions with it. The name Pignose? Well, we got ahold of some powerful hash and got into mixed metaphors.

Wayne (producer/director) got Steve Binder interested in promoting it; he paid for the copyright attorney and gave us enough to make about sixty-five Pignoses. At that time we were living in our storefront studio on Melrose Avenue in East Hollywood. We created "the legend" by giving away all of those original rubber-nosed amps to the top rock guitarists; naturally they all loved them. I moved to San Francisco; for one year I made experimental films and drove those motorized cable cars giving city tours. Wayne called me from LA with the news—he'd talked Jimmy Guercio (Chicago creator/producer) to fund the start-up of Pignose Industries, Inc. I came back to join him. We built the company, redesigned the original model 7-100, set up a production line, and got Martin Guitars to put it out to the market.

We gave away tens of thousands of 1½ inch diameter red, blue, and black on Mylar Pignose stickers; everywhere you went you'd see them stuck on everything. The first year, we made over 50,000 amps.

Premier

Premier Combo Twin 12 with beautiful tweed grill and handsome wood finishing

The World War II era also brought another amp maker to popularity, Premier manufactured by Multivox. Although they are handsome amps on the outside, interior wise, they weren't nearly as well made or reliable as Fender. Yet, many Blues guys tend to like these amps because of the warm overdrive they produce when their volume is pushed.

The Premier Combo Twin 12 gives that bluesy tone when you crank the volume.

Paul Reed Smith

Paul Reed Smith 25th Anniversary amp head: you gotta love that beautiful wood grain that PRS always uses on its instruments.

In recent years Paul Reed Smith has expanded into the amplifier market with the same quality and fervor as he did with his guitars. Now with a selection of combos, heads, and cabinets like the Archon, DG Custom, HXDA, and the 2 Channel Custom Series, Smith has joined the amp market in full force.

Here's Denny Jiosa with his 2 Channel "H" Paul Reed
Smith amp, ready to grab that tone.

Paul Reed Smith Sweet 16 single channel offers sixteen
watts of cathode-biased 6V6 output tubes.

Paul Reed Smith Archon, the heavyweight for high-gain overdrive

Quilter

The Quilter MicroPro 200 8 offers power and dynamic range for its size.

The man behind these amps is Pat Quilter, founder of QSC Audio Products. He uses a new technology called "switchmode design," also referred to as Class D. This new technology is much more complex and is typically used for applications in such widespread devices as cellphones and home theaters. Class D basically uses amplifying devices such as transistors like "Mosfets," for example, to operate as electronic switches, instead of as linear-gain devices in traditional amplifiers. This is the case of modern technology, integrated in amps to make them lighter weight and more affordable.

Roland

Roland is most famously synonymous with keyboards and drum machines, except for the Jazz

The Roland Cube-40GX can be linked to Apple's iPhone, iPad, and iPod touch with i-CUBE LINK.

The Quilter Aviator offers classic look and is lightweight.

Chorus JC-120 amp from the eighties. Who can forget those luscious chords of Andy Summers from the Police ringing out chorus chimes from the JC-120? From a personal perspective it never appealed to me coming from the overdriven school of tone; however, it was a very useful amp for some styles. Jazz cats, like Pat Methany, as well as new wave groups like the Cure and Siouxsie and the Banshees loved this amp. Even Zakk Wylde has a special place for this amp in his arsenal for recording clean tones.

Selmer

1964 Selmer Truvoice Treble-n-Bass 50, you can hear that warmth just from looking at it!

Selmer was a British distribution company that manufactured tube amps. During the sixties British Invasion, bands like the Beatles, the Animals, and the Shadows used Selmer amps. In 1928 a bloke by the name of Ben Davis established the Selmer Company in London. After World War II, Selmer purchased the company RSA/Truvoice, which specialized in making PA amplifiers. This put Selmar in the perfect place to start manufacturing guitar amps, and in the fifties, it started to produce the Truvoice models like the TV15 and TV6. From the early fifties to the seventies, Selmer also became the exclusive distributor for Höfner.

Seymour Duncan

Seymour Duncan is best known for outstanding guitar pickups; however, he made an amp called the Convertible back in the eighties that was fantastic. It had a built-in attenuator that went from five watts to 100 watts with a compartment on top that you could switch different tube modulars to achieve various tones. Each modular had a different tube in it like a 12AX7 or an ECC 83S that you could slip into various slots without having to rebias the amp. It was a wonderful way to experiment with tones

Seymour Duncan Convertible head, way ahead of its time with switchable pre-amp tubes

Seymour Duncan Convertible Amp, featuring channel switching, reverb, and attenuation control

and tubes on your own. This, of course, was way before THD amps were on the market.

Seymour Duncan Convertible tube modulars, Hi-Gain Hybrid, Presence, and Normal

Soldano

Around 1980 Mike Soldano started working on a guitar amplifier prototype that he named Mr. Science, which would have massive gain, parallel channels, and channel switching. Mike performed many a mod on Marshalls for his friends to get closer to his dream amp tone. In 1985 Mike started to make a name for himself in his

Soldano Reverb-O-Sonic sporting 4x10" speakers and two channels, which all controls go up to eleven!

hometown of Seattle among local guitarists. Then came the huge move to LA, where he set up shop in a former bordello. Mike reminisces, "We used to have guys come by to look at the amps and say, 'Where are the girls?'" Then things caught on when Heart guitarist Howard Leese purchased one of the first Soldano Amps. In turn Lou Reed and Vivian Campbell bought his amps, and by the

The Soldano Reverb-O-Sonic is one of the cleanest amp tones, but it can also deliver heavy overdrive—the perfect storm!

following year, he hit gold with Eric Clapton, the Scorpions, and Mark Knopfler representing his line of Soldano amps.

Sovtek

The Sovtek Midget 50H is one of the most underrated amps ever made, great overdrive tone!

Sovtek was the brainchild of Mike Matthews from Electro-Harmonix. In the 1980s when the

pedal market had dried up, Mike brought out the Sovtek amps. The "Amp Guru" Tony Bruno designed this amp by modifying a basic Fender amp. Mike recalls that he had orders for thousands of these amps, but the quality control was not up to par, and the potentiometers started to fall apart once on the market. I have to say, I own a MIG-50, and that thing sounds great and has exceptional tone. It is smaller than a Marshall, more like the size of a Fender Bassman, but it has a nice, fat overdrive tone when played through a 4x12" cabinet.

The Sovtek Midget 50H head has heavy tone that can compete with any Marshall.

Supro

The 1967 Supro Trojan reeks of vintage retro coolness.

The minute you hear the word Supro, automatically Jimi Hendrix and Jimmy Page come to mind. However, Supro has a long family tree, dating back to the twenties with National Reso-Phonic Guitars making resonator guitars. In the thirties Valco was formed when National and Dobro merged together. It was under the Valco name that Supro amps were developed and found an audience with blues men of the day because of their affordable prices. And of course the British Invasion guitarists who were so influenced by American blues naturally went out to get Supros. In case you were wondering, it was the Supro model 24 that Jimmy Page used on those first two Led Zeppelin records with a 1958 Fender Tele. I know right? It fooled me at first; I could swear Jimmy was playing a Les Paul through a Marshall stack.

Tone King Majesty 15, a tribute to the British tone of Plexi and JTM 45 tones

1965 Supro Thunderbolt, they've made a resurrection and are now being reissued by a US company.

Tone King

Mark Bartel started building amplifiers fairly early,

I had learned basic technician skills as a kid, helping my father fix old vacuum tube TVs, and that helped me get started in building electronic projects of my own. I initially built hi-fi power amps and pre-amps, but got involved with guitar amps after I started playing guitar in high school. At that point, my engineering knowledge was limited, so the amplifiers I was building were fairly crude. I started taking on repair work for local musicians and came across a lot of old vintage amps—mostly Fenders and Marshalls. This really helped me appreciate the sound of those amps and understand how they were built. I later went on to engineering school and worked in the semiconductor industry for many years, and that's where I developed the skills to do proper design and analysis from an engineer's perspective. By combining engineering knowledge with the technical and practical experience, I formed the design philosophy that I still use today.

So the natural course of events to happen was to open up his own business,

I started Tone King in 1993. At the time, there weren't many "boutique" amplifier companies around. I had a model called the Imperial, which I had designed for my own enjoyment. I hadn't necessarily intended to sell it commercially. After showing it around a bit, I found that players seemed to like it, and some were asking me to make one for them. Eventually, this led to starting the company. We're still selling that model today. There are a few things that I think make Tone King unique. The first is my approach to cabinet design. I learned early on that the speaker cabinet can have a huge impact on the sound of an amp and have spent many years experimenting to learn how certain factors of construction affect the tone, balance, feel, and sound field produced by a cabinet. I've built hundreds of test cabinets over the years, and I still seem to learn something new every time I design a new cabinet. When I develop a new amp, I spend at least as much time tuning the speaker cabinet as I do designing the electronics, and I like to think that this results in a certain unique synergy between the acoustic and electronic properties

Tone King Sky King powered by 6L6's with a built-in Ironman attenuator

of the amp. Another thing that I might consider unique is my approach to design work. As an engineer, I can draw out a circuit and optimize it's theoretical performance, but I also recognize that experimentation is very important to tuning an amp and will lead you to things that you may not have come across by engineering analysis alone. This is the "voodoo" that amps designers use in tweaking designs—things like varying component types/brands, wiring layout, etc. These types of "tweaks" are absolutely necessary to create the best possible design, but you need to keep in mind that any of these "voodoo" techniques must be explainable in terms of engineering principles. I'm not going to accept the premise that, say, green wire sounds better than red wire, when there's no reasonable explanation for that.

Mark enjoys the design process of amp building as he explains,

Whether it's a circuit design, cabinet design, etc. I'm always striving to take it further than I've gone before. I really enjoy the design process, and I'm driven to continue to learn and develop new ways of improving amp design. Regardless, to me "improving" doesn't mean creating new sounds; it's more a matter of digging deeper and getting closer to what makes vintage tones so great. The guitar tones I like are based in roots rock, classic rock, heavy metal, Motown, honky tonk, and old truck driver music. Most of what I do draws from that fixed canon of great guitar tones from the fifties through the eighties, but my approach is a little different than some designers. Instead of trying to duplicate a particular amp, I draw inspiration from certain characteristics of various vintage amp tones, deconstruct them to get to the core of what makes them so great, then create a design to get as close as possible to that ideal. It's more a matter of focusing on certain characteristics than on certain amps. For example, when I designed the Royalist amp, I was thinking of that early Plexi sound, Jeff Beck Group, Paul Kossoff with Free, etc. The sound I had in my head was likely an idealized amalgam of the tones on a lot of those classic tracks, and to me, was "better" than the sound I was getting when I plugged into a real vintage Plexi. I designed the Royalist to achieve that sound in my head, which I considered to be my own version of the "ideal plexi tone."

The Tone King Galaxy head features 4x6L6GC output stage (cathode biased), tweaked and voiced for chime.

Being a purist Mark has a certain opinion when it comes to digital-driven amps,

I spent many years doing digital-circuit design in industry, so I don't have an inherent bias against digital circuitry in general. Regardless, I just don't see a place for digital circuitry in the signal path of my kind of guitar amps. I'm always striving for purity in the signal path, the fewest possible components, the cleanest layout, etc., and obsessing over seemingly minor details of design and construction. I've seen cases where, for example, moving a certain component from one place on the chassis to another place, four inches away, had an audible effect. Digital modeling may be to the point where basic first- and second-order characteristics of devices (tubes, etc.) are being modeled, but as far as I know, it's nowhere near modeling a behavior like that.

Mark looks to the future with Tone King projects,

The design I'm currently working on started with a blank slate. The pre-amp, power amp, and other circuitry are entirely new, not even close to any existing design that I'm aware of. Regardless, it's not a modern design. If anything, it digs deeper than ever and recalls (my ideal version of) some funky old tones that haven't been around for quite a while. I think this is a good example of the way I work now and the way I expect to be working in five years. I like to innovate—I don't care to simply patch together building blocks taken from old vintage circuits. I suppose it's a bit ironic, I'm getting closer to vintage tones by doing things that haven't been done before.

Traynor

The Traynor Bass Master YBA-1 is also known as the poor man's Plexi.

It was in 1963 that music shop owner Jack Long and musician Pete Traynor formed the Yorkville Sound company in Canada. Its amps had the reputation for being built like tanks, which I can attest to—very hardy amp designs! Yorkville Sound is credited with installing a master volume in 1969, which pre-dates Marshall's master, which pre-dates Marshall's master-volume amps. Ironically, its bass amps were more suited for guitar. The YBA-1 Bass Master, I discovered, sounds fantastic when you jump the channels together and crank up the volume; this amp is also known as the poor man's Marshall Plexi. Because Yorkville introduced these amps as rentals, they were built to withstand the ultimate musician punishment. Timing is everything, and because of the explosion in North America with electrified instruments, many PA systems and amps were imported to America during the sixties. Such amps were: YGA-1 for guitar, the YVM-1 "Voice Master," a portable forty-five-watt tube amplifier, and the Dyna-Bass amp. Yorkville is still in business today and has introduced many amps such as the YCV20WR guitar amp, the AM Studio for acoustic guitar, the K2 for keyboards, and the YBA 300 for bass. This is a true testament of the quality and reliability of Yorkville's products.

Two-Rock

Two-Rock Amplification was cofounded by amp designer Bill Krinard and Joe Mloganoski in 1999. That same year, Carlos Santana bought the Two-Rock number 5 amp, which was tweaked into tonal shape by Bill. Since then, it has made amps for Brad Whitford from Aerosmith, John Scofield, blues-rock guitarist Joe Bonamassa, and Eric Gales. Two-Rock prides itself as an artisan, hand wiring everything point to point.

Two-Rock EXO-15, powered by 2-6V6, tube rectified and with contour control

Watkins

This is the story of another British entrepreneur who captured the moment diligently with an amplifier. Charlie Watkins served in World War II and, after coming back home to a war-torn London, opened up a record store. By the fifties that peculiar British craze of the "Skiffle" took hold, and everyone wanted a guitar and amp. Just Google "Skiffle," and you'll find a video of a very young Jimmy Page playing guitar on a London TV show. It just simply puts a big smile on my face. Right, now back to good ole Charlie. He started to import German instruments to sell in England and then with the help of Arthur O'Brien designed the Westminster, the Clubman, and the flagship Dominator with a Vox-like voicing using EL84s

The Two-Rock Studio Pro Plus features mucho headroom and adjustable EQ settings

The 1963 Watkins Dominator is absolutely retro sixties; let's watch the Ed Sullivan Show!

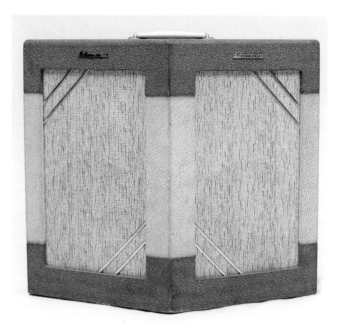

The 1963 Watkins Dominator is powered by two EL84s with a real "cool factor" emanating from it.

for power tubes. Then in 1958 Charlie hit upon something that really caught the ears of the British youths, a tube-powered tape-echo machine called "The Copicat." In fact from the early 2000s until his death in 2014, Charlie resurrected the business by reissuing the Copicat and the Dominator, along with other musical instruments from his heyday.

Attenuators

Weber Mass 100 Watt, simply the best amplifier attenuator on the market, with built-in speaker motor for a more natural effect

This is the age-old question since the dawn of rock 'n' roll: how can you get that sweet spot in the

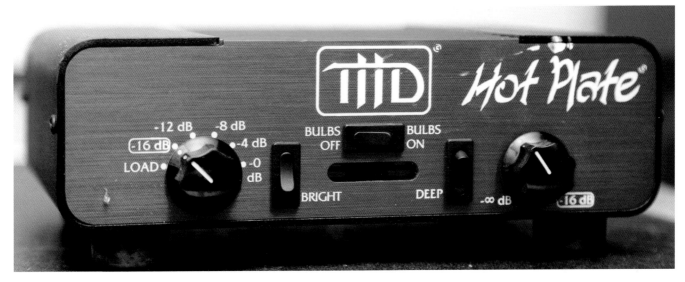

THD 8 Ohm Hot Plate, with various controls for db reduction

amp without blowing everyone's ears out? Well, the first answer is to create some sort of master volume. However, doing so does change the overall tone, because the speaker cabinet is not working as hard, and therefore the speakers aren't moving as much air. This actually does matter and sounds different from cranking it wide open. Some addressed it by making smaller-watt amps, but still the tone is different. Just think of the Jimi Hendrix tone at Woodstock; man, that is simply one of the best tones I ever heard. A buddy of mine, who attended the show, said you could hear it for miles around. Even in the studio, his tone didn't sound as good as Woodstock, because he wasn't cranked up as loud. The one company who has nailed it is Weber, and it hosts an array of attenuators. It actually has a very well-built product that contains an actual speaker motor that applies a reactive load on the amp. Some other models on the market squash the tone, because they are resistor based. Hence you get much more of a natural tone from the amp, as if you were cranking it completely wide open. The Weber models also contain detail controls of Tone Stack for bass, middle, and treble frequencies. There is an impedance-control knob, as well as a treble-boost switch.

The company THD Electronics also offers an array of attenuators called Hot Plates that are very good as well. The device is comprised of capacitors, resistors, and inductors that are volume sensitive. So as the overall volume of the amp is adjusted, the Hot Plate compensates for the human ear's frequency response. According to the company's website, "Your ear perceives sounds differently at different volumes: the louder the sound, the more sensitive your ears are to highs and lows. As the

Jet City Jettenuator, a hand-wired 100-watt attenuator with many features

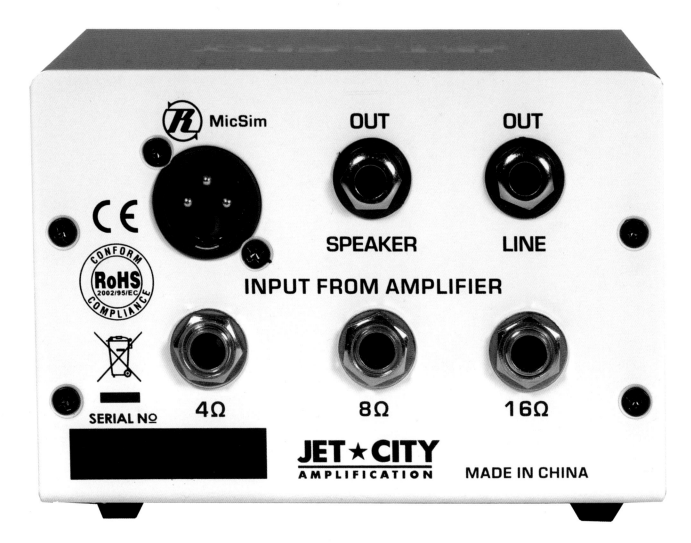

Jet City Jettenuator rear panel, featuring a variety of connections

volume drops, your ear becomes more sensitive to the mid-range and less so for highs and lows. The Hot Plate compensates for this, working like the 'Loudness' switch on a hi-fi. The THD Hot Plate is the first and, for now, the only attenuator that is frequency compensated."

With that technical stuff being said, the proof is in the pudding. I use a Hot Plate on my MESA/Boogie Mark IIB, and it sounds great and does what it's supposed to do. Other companies that manufacture attenuators well are our friends at Jet City Amplification, Marshall, and Radial.

Bibliography

bibliography bibliography bibliography bibliography

The Tube Amp Book by Aspen Pittman
Backbeat Books (September 1, 2003)

Fender Amps: The First Fifty Years by John Teagle and John Sprung
Hal Leonard Publishing Corporation (July 1995)

Jim Marshall the Father of Loud: The Story of the Man Behind the World's Most Famous Amp by Rich Maloof
and Jim Marshall
Backbeat Books (December 1, 2003)

Amps!: The Other Half of Rock 'N' Roll by Ritchie Fliegler
Hal Leonard Publishing (November 1993)

The Official Vintage Guitar Magazine Price Guide by Alan Greenwood and Gil Hembree
Vintage Guitar Books (October 2013)

365 Guitars, Amps & Effects You Must Play: The Most Sublime, Bizarre and Outrageous Gear Ever by Dave Hunter
Voyageur Press (May 15, 2013)

Index

F

 **Books from Allworth Press**

Allworth Press is an imprint of Skyhorse Publishing, Inc. Selected titles are listed below.

The Art of Writing Great Lyrics
by Pamela Phillips Oland (6 x 9, 272 pages, paperback, $18.95)

Guitar Encyclopedia
by Brian Tarquin (8 ½ x 11, 256 pages, paperback, $29.95)

How Music Dies (or Lives)
by Ian Brennan (6 x 9, 426 pages, paperback, $19.99)

How to Grow as a Musician
by Sheila E. Anderson (6 x 9, 256 pages, paperback, $22.95)

The Insider's Guide to Home Recording
by Brian Tarquin (5 ½ x 8 ½, 224 pages, paperback, $16.95)

The Insider's Guide to Music Licensing
by Brian Tarquin (6 x 9, 256 pages, paperback, $19.95)

Making and Marketing Music
by Jodi Summers (6 x 9, 240 pages, paperback, $19.95)

Making It in the Music Business
by Lee Wilson (6 x 9, 256 pages, paperback, $24.95)

Managing Artists in Pop Music
by Mitch Weiss and Perri Gaffney (6 x 9, 288 pages, paperback, $19.95)

Profiting from Your Music and Sound Project Studio
by Jeffrey Fisher (6 x 9, 224 pages, paperback, $24.95)

Rock Star 101
by Marc Ferrari (6 x 9, 176 pages, paperback, $17.95)

The Songwriter's and Musician's Guide to Nashville
by Sherry Bond (6 x 9, 256 pages, paperback, $19.95)

To see our complete catalog or to order online, please visit *www.allworth.com*.